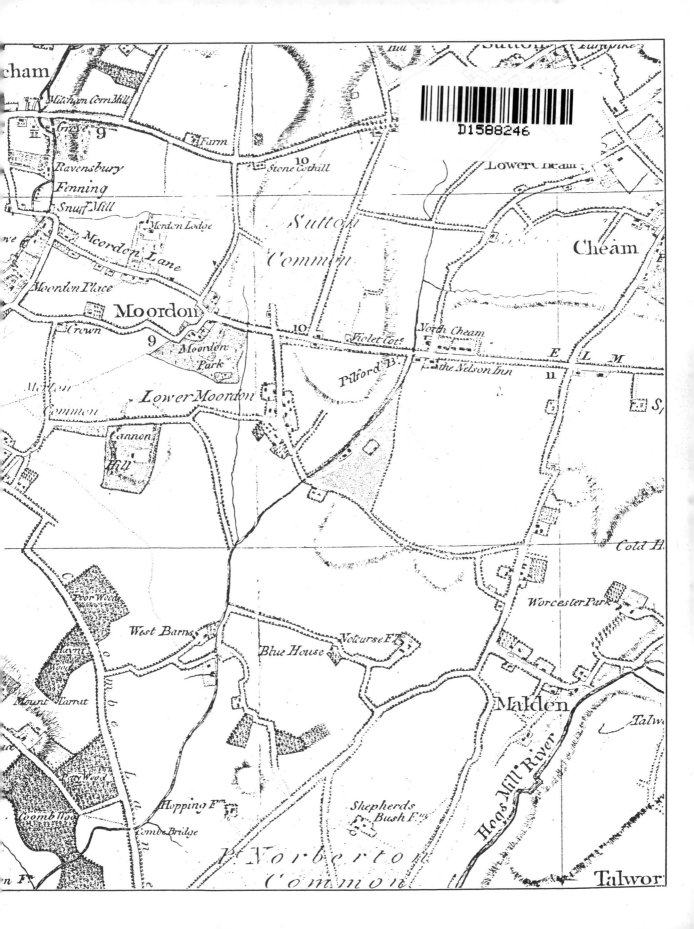

MERTON AND MORDEN
A Pictorial History

Armorial bearings of Merton and Morden. In 1943 Merton and Morden District Council applied to the College of Arms for a grant of arms. The Wandsworth and District Gas Company presented the council with an oil painting of the bearings to hang in the council chamber. The heraldic description is: *Sable a fret or on a Chief of the last two Lions passant respectant of the Field*. The fret is derived from the arms of Merton Priory, which held lands in Merton between 1121 and 1538. The two lions are taken from the arms of the Garth family, lords of the manor of Morden from 1553 to 1872. The motto 'In libertate vis' or 'Strength in freedom' was chosen as especially appropriate in wartime.

[illustration from *Merton and Morden Official Guide, c.*1957, pub. Ed.J. Burrow & Co. Ltd.]

MERTON AND MORDEN
A Pictorial History

Judith Goodman

Phillimore

1995

Published by
PHILLIMORE & CO. LTD.,
Shopwyke Manor Barn, Chichester, West Sussex

ISBN 1 86077 007 X

Printed and bound in Great Britain by
BIDDLES LTD.
Guildford, Surrey

To Sarah, Tim and Richard

MORDEN HALL PARK-BARN. OVER 500 YEARS OLD
DESTROYED BY FIRE

List of Illustrations

Frontispiece: Armorial bearings of Merton and Morden

Acknowledgements

My thanks are due to Penny Parker and the London Borough of Merton Library Service for the generous access to material which has been allowed to me; to all the library staff for their help, particularly to Wendy Siemaszko, Information Team Librarian at Morden Reference Library, for her interest and endless patience; to colleagues in the John Innes Society and Merton Historical Society, especially to Bill Rudd, Geoffrey Wilson and John Wallace, who so generously shared their knowledge of the history of Merton and Morden; to Ken Glazier who kindly clarified some transport matters; and to my husband Michael who took just the right amount of interest—and let me monopolise the study for many months.

The illustrations are reproduced with kind permission from the following sources: Roland Benbow, 124; The Bodleian Library, University of Oxford, 1; Douglas Braid, 40; The British Library, 83; Croydon Advertiser Group Ltd., 59, 126, 176; John Gent, 21, 66, 69, 95, 100, 133, 134, 166; Greater London Record Office, 42, 91, 114, 136, 137; Imperial War Museum, 158-62; John Innes Archives, John Innes Centre, 34, 35, 115, 156; John Innes Society, 5, 20, 22, 24-7, 30-3, 38, 64, 65, 81, 84, 85, 87-9, 93, 98, 116, 118, 129, 151, 157, 163; Church of St Lawrence, Morden, 52; Leighton House, Royal Borough of Kensington and Chelsea, 13; London Transport Museum, 71-3, 75, 76; Merton Libraries Department, 2-4, 9-11, 14-6, 18, 19, 23, 28, 29, 36, 37, 39, 41, 43-9, 51, 53-8, 60-3, 67, 68, 70, 74, 77-80, 82, 86, 92, 94, 96, 104-10, 119-23, 127, 130, 132, 135, 138-40, 142-50, 152-4, 164, 165, 167-75, 177-83; Stephen Morgan, 97; William Morris Gallery, London Borough of Waltham Forest, 103; Royal London Hospital Archives and Museum, 101; Bill Rudd, 111, 112; Sotheby's, 7, 8; Wimbledon Society, 6, 12, 17, 90, 99, 102, 117, 128, 131, 141, 155; Author's collection, frontispiece, 50, 113, 125.

Early Times

The geology of Merton and Morden consists mainly of London Clay, which is about 50 million years old, overlain in places by gravel river terraces, laid down in the Ice Ages. Near the River Wandle are some more recent alluvial deposits. Early man would have found the area well forested, and probably offering good hunting—mammoth bones have been found in Morden, and palaeolithic (Old Stone Age) handaxes in Kingston Road. However settlement and cultivation were late here, because, except on the gravels, drainage was poor and the heavy clay could not be worked properly before the introduction of the improved Saxon plough.

The 'mound' in Morden Park, perhaps of Roman date, perhaps older, remains a mystery until proper investigation, but the largest archaeological feature in the district is Stane Street, the road built by the Romans from Chichester to London. This enters Morden at Stonecot Hill, where modern and ancient road coincide briefly, and then cuts through part of Morden Park, where its course has been picked up at a few points. Between there and Colliers Wood High Street its precise route is still conjectural, though its Wandle crossing is likely to have been at or near the present point, for late in the 19th century Roman masonry was said to have been found in the fabric of the bridge. There was probably a 'mansio' or staging station in Merton or Morden, and Romano-British pottery, tiles and coins have been found locally.

Despite the presence of a large Saxon cemetery in Mitcham, little has been found in Merton and Morden from the Saxon period. However, the Domesday Survey of 1086 tells us that by that date there were established settlements. Merton, whose name, sometimes written then as Meretone or Meretune, probably means 'farmstead by the pool', had belonged to Earl Harold and passed with the Conquest into the hands of the Norman king. It was rated at 20 hides, a hide being a variable measurement of ploughed land—here perhaps 50 hectares (120 acres). Morden (Mordune or Mordone), or 'hill in a swampy place', remained with its pre-Conquest owners, Westminster Abbey, and was valued at three hides. Merton had a church and two mills. At Morden there was a mill, but no church is mentioned.

The inhabitants of the two small communities ploughed the fields with teams of oxen, grew wheat for bread, barley for ale, and a few food crops; in the manorial woods they fed their pigs and gathered wood. In Merton there were 56 villeins (villagers) and 13 bordars; Morden had eight villeins and five cottars. The two different words for the lowly cottage-dweller who had to hire his labour out to survive may derive from the fact that Merton and Morden were in different 'hundreds' (administrative divisions)— Merton in Brixton and Morden in Wallington.

In 1114 Henry I gave the 'vill' of Merton to Gilbert the Knight, a distinguished and pious man, who had been sheriff of Surrey. After building a church, probably of wood, on the site of the present one, Gilbert was granted a licence by the king to establish a monastery in Merton. The first wooden building is believed to have been near the church, but soon a new site was chosen beside the Wandle, where on 25 hectares

(60 acres) a fine stone church was built, together with domestic quarters and other buildings, for a community of Canons Regular of St Augustine. In 1121 the Priory (and, though it became rich and powerful, it was never an abbey) was granted the manor of Merton. While proving to be an exacting landlord, and sometimes negligent in such duties as alms-giving, the Priory played host to royalty, as well as scholars and statesmen. It is possible that both Thomas Becket and the founder of Merton College, Walter de Merton, were educated there. A great council held in the large chapter house in 1236 enacted the Statutes of Merton.

The Priory may have been an occasional source of employment for the people of Merton and have given them a glimpse of the wider world; but Morden, remote from its Westminster lords, continued its quiet life, its affairs administered by a bailiff, its rectory appropriated by the Abbey, its people struggling for subsistence.

1   The charter of King Edgar A.D. 967. By the mid-10th century Merton had become a royal 'vill'. King Edgar (957-75) rewarded his loyal *comes* (earl) Aelfeah, and his wife Aelfswith, with 20 *cassata* of land in Merton, together with smaller parcels in Dulwich and near the Thames. A *cassata* was about 48 hectares (120 acres). The grant was free of all taxes except those of military service by the inhabitants and the maintenance of bridges and defences. This 14th-century copy of a lost 10th-century document is mainly in Latin, but gives the bounds of the Merton estate in English, including *hidebourne* (an old name of the Wandle) and *hoppinge* (a name surviving until recently in that of Hopping Wood, Malden). The text begins at the large word 'Mertone' and continues on the right-hand page. It is followed by a charter of A.D. 949, in which King Eadred granted land at Merton to Wulfric, but it is not known if this was the Surrey Merton, nor has this Wulfric been identified. [Bodleian Library, MS Wood, empt.I, fols. 228v-229r]

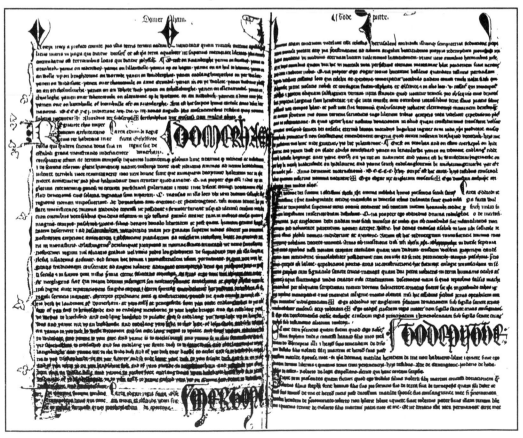

The Old Villages

On John Rocque's maps made in the mid-18th century there are few roads to be seen in the old parishes. From the Wandle crossing to Stonecot Hill ran a stretch of the highway from London to Epsom and beyond. Leaving it at what came to be called Merton Grove was the ancient route to Kingston, which after a mile took two sharp bends before curving north-west to the Coombe crossing of the Beverley Brook. There were lanes that would become Morden Hall Road and Central Road, Church Lane and Church Path, a few tracks near Merton Rush, a farm-road to West Barnes, footpaths and trackways giving access to the commons, and little else. Small clusters of dwellings were scattered here and there—by the industrial sites on the Wandle, along the Kingston Road, near the parish churches, and around the inns. There were a few large houses, some of them in substantial estates.

Following the dissolution of the Priory in 1538 the site began to be plundered for building material, for Henry VIII's Nonsuch Palace at Ewell and for many humbler edifices. All that can be seen at 'Merton Abbey' today are some short stretches of boundary wall and some remains of the chapter house. The rebuilt entrance arch of the Priory guest-house stands in St Mary's churchyard. With the dissolution the manor of Merton reverted to the Crown, but from early in the 17th century it was held by a succession of secular lords, by no means all resident, the longest ownership being that by the Dorrills from 1693 to 1802. Leasehold estates, set up even before the dissolution, were a feature of Merton, which became a setting for the country residences of London merchants and officials.

In Morden the Garths were lords of the manor from 1554 to 1872, the inheritance twice passing through the female line, so that the heirs had to assume the name of Garth. Although for much of that time the family was not resident, this continuity lent a stability to life in Morden. No long leases of Garth land were granted until a private Act of Parliament was passed in 1768, when the Morden Park estate was created by John Ewart, a London merchant. This quiet village, conveniently near London, began to be a country retreat of men such as George Hoare of the banking family and Sir Joseph Bazalgette, engineer of London's main drainage system.

Bricks and tiles were made of local clay. Building stone could come from Reigate or Merstham, by cart or, in the early 19th century, most of the way on the Surrey Iron Railway. More modest houses had tile-hung upper storeys and boarding below, to keep out the weather. Some cottages were built entirely of timber, painted white. Barns were of tarred timber—one such survived in Morden Hall Park from the 17th century until burnt down in 1991. Flint, brought from the North Downs, was used sometimes—at St Mary the Virgin, in the much rebuilt fragments of the Priory walls, in farm buildings at Bakers End.

Unlike their neighbours at Mitcham and Wimbledon, the people of Merton and Morden lost their commons in the 19th century. Ironically, it was one of the Statutes of Merton of 1236 that entitled the lord of a manor to enclose the common for his own use, provided enough was left for tenants with common rights, such as grazing. This was a situation open to abuse. John Hilbert of Wandsworth, who bought the manor of Merton in 1802, obtained an Act of Parliament in 1816 permitting him to enclose, despite brave resistance led by parson and vestry, and the whole common was broken up into plots. The area it once covered was roughly triangular, with its base at Cannon Hill Lane, and bisected by what is now Martin Way.

Morden common, a triangular remnant of a much larger expanse once known as Sparrowfield, lay in the south-west corner of the parish, beyond and bordered by the Pyl Brook. It was too remote to be much used for grazing, and early enclosures were accepted without protest. In 1885 Gilliat Hatfeild sold parts of it, which already held a market garden, a brickworks, and a number of houses, though some open ground here survived to the 1920s.

There was a pound for stray animals in Kingston Road, where the Manor Club stands, and one at the corner of Morden churchyard.

In both parishes charities helped the poor with clothes, bread or coal. The 17th-century Rowland Wilson almshouses in Kingston Road once housed six poor men or women. The last remnant of it was pulled down in 1968, but the almshouse founded for poor women by Elizabeth Simon of Spring House at the end of the 18th century still stands in Kingston Road.

2 The exact site of this quaint group of ramshackle cottages at Merton has not yet been located, but they are probably typical of the dwellings of the better-off local labourers or small farmers over several centuries.

3 With its three floors and jettied construction, this is a substantial pair of cottages, and could possibly be the building that once stood at the corner of Church Lane and Kingston Road, Merton, before old Dorset Lodge was built.

4 'Rats' Castle' in 1909. A rear view of what was once a workshop or storehouse at Mr. Jacob's whitster (calico bleaching) grounds in Phipps Bridge Road. In 1805 it was a barn with stables, and when this photograph was taken it seems to have become a combined dwelling and shop, for at the front it displayed a Batey's lemonade advertisement. Its nickname suggests that it was not a salubrious building.

5 Sutton's Cottages, Church Path, *c*.1920. This building stood end-on to the road, roughly where St Mary's parish office is now. It is believed to have been in existence by 1538, and when the illegitimate daughter of William Head, who farmed at Bakers End, married William Sutton in 1828, it was part of her marriage settlement. Before it was condemned and pulled down *c*.1958, it had become decidedly ramshackle, with daffodils sprouting in the thatch each spring. The last occupant, who lived without piped water, drains or electricity, acted as caretaker of the old church hall, of which one corner of the roof can be seen jutting out beyond the cottages.

6 Sutton's Cottages, Cannon Hill Lane, 1913. These early 19th-century cottages, built on the west side of the lane, belonged to Mr. Head, a farmer at Bakers End, and were part of his daughter Mary Sutton's marriage settlement. They stood close to where the Wimbledon-Sutton railway now crosses the road and survived until the local council's housing development of 1923. In the background at the right are some of the early 20th-century houses that face the recreation ground pavilion.

7 & 8 Morden Hall, *c.*1790, was built by the Garths to the north of their old manor house, known as Growtes, in the middle of the 18th century. At first they lived here, but it was soon leased out, and these attractive drawings by John Wells date from the tenancy of Thomas Sainsbury towards the end of the century. Illustration 7 shows the north front, with its central canted bay which looked onto one arm of the 'moat', and the pastures beyond. From the south-east (illustration 8) the main front of the house can be seen, showing a colonnade between the projecting wings. Two more arms of the 'moat' are shown. Many new trees appear to have been planted, apparently informally, and the tall trees in the background look like elms edging the lane that became Morden Hall Road.

9 James Lackington the London bookseller. He took up residence in 1791 at Spring House, built *c*.1726 and situated at an angle to Kingston Road, nearly opposite Church Lane. Lackington became rich by buying up libraries and publishers' 'remainders' for sale at his famous shop in Finsbury Square, known as the Temple of the Muses. He it was who called Upper Merton 'the most rural village in Surrey', and, though he still went up to London three or four times a week, he liked to wander in Merton's fields with a book in his hand. Lackington's second wife, Dorcas, is buried in the churchyard beneath a florid epitaph composed by her husband. This portrait is the frontispiece from the 13th edition of his popular *Memoirs*. It is thought that, after Lackington's departure, Spring House was the setting of the idyllic summer described by Leigh Hunt in his *Autobiography*, during which, as a boy of 12 or 13, he explored, bathed in the Wandle, and fell in love.

10 Merton Place, *c*.1806. A whimsical view of 'Paradise Merton', as Emma Hamilton described it to her lover, Lord Nelson. It was his 'dear, dear Merton'. The former Moat Farm had been rebuilt about 1780 by Sir Richard Hotham and Nelson bought it for Emma in 1801. She added a new wing and chose the lavish furniture and decorations for which it became notorious. After Nelson's death in 1805 Emma fell into financial difficulties and in 1808 had to sell the house. By 1823 it had been demolished and the estate was auctioned as building plots. Only the names of local streets and pubs are reminders now of England's hero. The site of the house is south of the High Street, almost opposite Victory Road.

11 Morden Lodge, 1806. Abraham Goldsmid's house was just completed when this view was drawn. A member of a Dutch Jewish family, Goldsmid ran one of London's great broking houses. He chose Morden for his country seat and built this striking house, with a main saloon the full height of the roof. The principal rooms were decorated by the firm of Crace & Sons, who had worked at the Royal Pavilion, Brighton. Notice the aloes in wheeled tubs on the lawn, part of the exotic atmosphere of the place.

At the first reception here, in September 1806, the 300 guests included the Prince of Wales, two royal dukes, Richard Brinsley Sheridan, playwright and politician, and Sir Robert Burnett, of the Vauxhall Distillery, who lived next door at Morden Hall. Lesser local gentry were invited for the later part of the evening and were entertained with music indoors and spectacle outdoors, with thousands of lamps in the trees.

In 1810 society and the markets were shaken by the news that Goldsmid had shot himself here in the grounds. Depressed by the death of Sir Francis Baring, his partner in a £14 million loan to the Government, he was believed to have despaired when 'omnium', Government stock, began to fall. It is thought that this house was never lived in again. In the 1820s it was pulled down and the present Morden Lodge built.

12 Long Lodge, 1826. Edward Hassell's drawing of Long Lodge dates from the ownership of Ann Caroline Blakiston, and shows the house looking very much as it does today. The central portion is the oldest and dates from c.1720. Additions were made c.1750 (to the left) and c.1785 (to the right), and it has three staircases. Note the six windows on the right that have been bricked up, probably to reduce window tax. Although Kingston Road has been widened and straightened since this view was drawn, artistic licence has given the garden greater depth than it can have had even then.

13 Frederic Shields, *above left*, lived at Long Lodge in Kingston Road from 1895 until his death in 1911. A minor but interesting member of the Pre-Raphaelite circle, he was particularly close to Dante Gabriel Rossetti. Shields built a studio in the grounds, which were then still thickly planted with trees, but though he had moved to Merton to escape from noise and disturbance he did not find Long Lodge a peaceful haven. It is perhaps fortunate that he did not live to see the first motor buses pass his door. This portrait in enamels is by Ernestine Mills, his protégée and biographer, and a frequent visitor to Merton.

14 The Kennels, Lower Morden Lane, 1937, *above right*. Despite the name it was pigs that were raised here in living memory. The construction of the house may suggest a surviving wing of a hall-house. Notice the jettied upper storey. The Kennels burned down in 1937.

15 Cottages in Lower Morden Lane, 1937, *below*. A rear view of a group of farm cottages which stood near what was once called Morden Green, close to the present Beverley roundabout and roughly opposite Bow Lane. Perhaps 200 years old by the date of this view, they were about to be pulled down for part of the 'Morden Park' estate which was being developed. In the mid-19th century the building on the right may have been the beerhouse known at different dates as the *Jolly Farmers* and the *Sheepshearers*.

16 Ravensbury Farm buildings, Wandle Road. Ravensbury farmhouse was not the present house of the name, but is believed to be the house that survives on the west corner of Wandle Road and Morden Hall Road. However these buildings lay between Wandle Road and the river but have now been replaced by housing.

17 Nos. 122-4 Kingston Road, 1913. A typical weatherboard building, with pantiled roof, which housed Howell's laundry and 'Large open air Drying Grounds' behind. In the one-time Merton Farm next door, a late 17th-century construction but with a later façade, George C. Wood & Sons ran their building business for many years, as tenants of the local council. Now known as Manor House, it has been converted to office suites. The cottages have gone.

18 Littler's or White Cottage, 1963. A late view of this old (now vanished) weatherboard cottage by the Wandle, and off Phipps Bridge Road. It had been built by 1805 and was later owned by the Littler family, textile printers, and lived in by at least one of them for a time in the 19th century.

19 The Laurels, Central Road, was one of a handful of substantial, though incongruously urban-looking, villas which were built in Morden in Victorian days. Before the last war Mrs. Annie Ida Edwards ran a kindergarten and preparatory school here. The Laurels survived at least until the 1950s, beside St George's church, but has since been replaced by a block of flats of the same name.

20 Dorset Lodge, Kingston Road, was built *c*.1835 and later enlarged and altered, probably by H.G. Quartermain. It stood on the east corner with Church Lane where it formed a 'pinch' in the main road and was a notorious traffic hazard, despite its curved corner! Occupants in the 19th century included the retired workhouse master, Thomas Bowen, and James Matthias, who preceded John Innes as lord of the manor. The last owner was Dr. Raymond Harvey, who demolished it in 1951 and replaced it with a new Dorset Lodge set safely back from the road.

Top of George Hill, Morden. 6264.

21 The top of George Hill from a postcard view sold by Ernest Chennell at his shop near the *Crown*. The horse trough at the junction of Central Road with London Road was the gift of Miss Juliette Reckitt in 1906, 'in memory of the horses that suffered in the South African War', and cost £60 17s. 9d. When the main road was widened and straightened in the 1970s, it was moved at Canon Livermore's request to a site outside the church on the other side of London Road. On the right is the old schoolhouse, and on the left is one of the pair of Church Cottages, which were demolished to make way for the road-widening.

22 The Village Club and Reading Room was situated on the corner of Crown Road and London Road, Morden. It was established by 1890 and used for meetings, billiards, social events and adult classes. In the little row of shops was Chennell's general shop and post office, a sweet shop, a baker, and a greengrocer, and beyond the old *Plough* in the distance stood two cottages and a forge.

Growth of the Surburbs

The arrival in the early 1860s of the 23 Fairlawn Villas (now Nos 209-53 Kingston Road), built by William Blackford, prosperous son of a Wimbledon bootmaker, must have startled the people of Merton. But occupants were soon found, mostly business or professional people, newcomers on the whole, who were likely to look towards London for their livelihoods, and who were not deterred by a muddy walk to Wimbledon station—Hartfield Road was not made up until a few years later.

With the arrival in Merton *c.*1865 of John Innes, a City property developer, the next stage began. Innes, with his brother James, bought Manor Farm in Watery Lane from John Hilbert Tate, lord of the manor of Merton, and Morden Hall Farm from Richard Garth, lord of the manor of Morden. Further purchases soon followed, enabling the Innes brothers to lay out Mostyn and Dorset Roads. John Innes made his home at Manor Farm; villas and cottages began to go up here and there, and Innes took on Henry Goodall Quartermain as estate architect.

For nearly forty years Innes developed Merton Park, as he named his estate, with houses of varied size and design in leafy avenues, often bordered with holly hedges. But despite its attractions the estate failed to grow as fast as he perhaps expected; the southern extent, including chestnut-lined Kenley Road, would remain empty for more than twenty years after the deaths in 1904 of both Innes and Quartermain.

From the 1880s some imposing houses had been going up in Grand Drive. And, around the turn of the century, at Bushey Mead and at the southern end of West Barnes Lane intensive development started. The Polytechnic Estate, west of Merton Hall Road, followed from the turn of the century, and then the 'station estate' between the railway line and Morden Road. Sydney Brocklesby built a range of charming Arts and Crafts villas for the Merton Park Estate Company, as well as buildings for the Horticultural Institution, and for the John Innes Park and Recreation Ground.

Merton's population, which had grown between 1801 and 1901 from 800 to 4,500, more than doubled again by 1907, when it became an Urban District. But meanwhile Morden had grown only from about 500 in 1801 to under 1,000 at the end of the century, and an estimated 1,100 in 1907. Although Stanley, Crown and Queen's Roads were built up around 1900 with small houses, and there was a development of villas on large plots in Pollard Road on the Ravensbury Park estate, Morden remained truly a village well into the 20th century.

After the standstill in building during the First World War, and the severe housing shortage which followed, various Small Homes Acquisitions Acts came into force, and the district council bought the Whatley estate in 1920 to build subsidised housing. Five years later George Blay began to develop the Cannon Hill estate, and the old Raynes Park golf course was built up in the same way. More roads at Ravensbury Park were laid out and developed, partly with self-built houses and bungalows. The opening in

1926 of the Underground extension to Morden was the spur to the long-delayed southern development of John Innes's land, including 'Merton Park Estate No. 2', south of Martin Way. The last remnants of Blagdon's and Blue House Farms, between the Beverley and Pyl Brooks, disappeared, and towards Coombe Bridge the farm fields became sports grounds interspersed with new avenues.

However, the most dramatic change came in 1926-9, when 130 hectares (322 acres) of land in Morden were acquired, mostly by compulsory purchase, as part of the London County Council's St Helier Estate. By 1939 more than 3,500 new dwellings had been built on this land and Morden was completely transformed.

23 Abbey Road. When Nelson's Merton Place was sold off for housing in 1823 a development known as Nelson's Fields rapidly grew up—narrow roads, cramped housing and small businesses. This undated view looking north towards the High Street could, with its cloaked female figures, easily be in the London slums or the industrial north.

24 The Manor House, 1899. John Innes bought the old Manor Farm in Watery Lane in about 1868, and employed H.G. Quartermain to alter and enlarge it to this substantial dwelling. It is said that the builders worked here, on and off, for 30 years. Ornamental grounds were laid out, with conservatories and a 'grotto' adjoining the house. Between the wars it was occupied by the director of the John Innes Horticultural Institution, and today the building serves as part of Rutlish High School.

25 Leigh Villas, situated next to the level crossing in Kingston Road, had only just been built when this photograph was taken *c*.1870 and are typical of the early houses of John Innes's Merton Park. The house on the right was the estate office and first local home of H.G. Quartermain, the principal architect to the estate. Rather oddly, the house second from the left advertises itself to let—rent free!

26 Dewhurst, seen here *c.*1895, stands on the west corner of Kingston Road and Church Lane. It was built in 1885 to designs by Quartermain and it exhibits some of the architect's favourite touches—balconies with Chinese-style balustrades, an oriel window, a blank *œuil-de-bœuf*, tile-hung gables and decorative brick-work. A hundred years ago the elm trees of Church Lane lent a rural touch to the view. The house is now part of a retirement development.

27 Gardeners' Cottage in Watery Lane was brand new when this view was taken in 1899 and was built to house John Innes's unmarried gardening staff. Here they were looked after by a housekeeper. In the background are cottages at the Rush. A few years later Manor Gardens was laid out, cutting through the hedge at the left.

28 A view of Grand Drive in 1911, looking south from Blenheim Road. The road was laid out by Richard Garth all the way to Lower Morden *c*.1870, but in the early days it was not maintained, and where it crossed the Raynes Park golf course its condition deteriorated to that of a muddy footpath.

29 West Barnes Lane, *c*.1910, looking north-west towards West Barnes crossing. The cottage on the right was built before 1891 by Charles Blake, the local landowner, and was then known as Concrete Cottage, but after 1913, more euphoniously, as Chestnut Cottage. The houses opposite stood between Phyllis (named after the developer's daughter) and Adela Avenues and had only just been built when this photograph was taken.

30 The stretch of land south of the The Chase, west of Merton Hall Road and north of Kingston Road had been a sports field used by the Regent Street Polytechnic, founded by Quintin Hogg in the 1880s. It was sold for housing at the beginning of the 20th century and a series of parallel avenues was built up sporadically in an attractive development by the Polytechnic Estate Company. In this view of Kingston Road, *c*.1910, are Estate houses and shops of *c*.1903, including a bakery on the corner of Quintin Avenue. In the distance are the shops of Merton Park Parade, built *c*.1907, and the trees on the right mark Blakesley and its garden.

31 Kirkley Road, *c*.1910. The 'station estate' was developed on the north-east side of the LBSCR Wimbledon-Tooting line. Under the management of estate agents Edwin Evans & Co. several builders were involved, and a number of styles, with variations within styles, can be identified. Kirkley Road dates from 1905, but its original name of Rostrevor Road was changed at the request of the post office, as there was already a road of that name in Wimbledon.

32 Dorset Hall was built in the reign of Queen Anne and much altered in the 1830s. It was the home of Thomas and Rose Lamartine Yates, its last private owners, when this photograph was taken in 1912. They sometimes opened the fine gardens for the local flower show, but looked to Wimbledon and London for social contact. He was a solicitor in Chancery Lane and she was best known for her work as a Suffragette—as Organising Secretary of the Wimbledon Women's Social and Political Union. This news agency photograph dates from the occasion when the national Suffragette leader, Christabel Pankhurst, evaded arrest by disappearing. Before it was discovered that she had gone to Paris, Dorset Hall was one location where she was (incorrectly) thought to be sheltering.

33 On 29 June 1912 a garden reception was held at Dorset Hall in honour of three Suffragette ex-prisoners (two are seated, and the third is in the hammock) who had been on hunger-strike. Rose Lamartine Yates stands fourth from the right, Thomas stands on the extreme right, and their four-year-old son Paul kneels beside the hammock. Rose herself had served one month in prison for 'obstruction' when Paul was a baby.

34 Under the terms of John Innes's will a horticultural institution was set up in 1910 in his Manor House grounds, and his ornamental garden became the John Innes Park. This view looks across farm fields destined to become the plant trial grounds, from Mostyn Road to Cannon Hill Lane, where new speculative housing, by Mr. Coombs of Broadwater House, can be seen in the distance, beyond the elm trees.

35 John Innes Horticultural Institution buildings. Local architect Sydney Brocklesby designed a number of buildings for the institution including this workshop and the 'superintendent's house' near the main entrance in Mostyn Road. Both buildings are now used by Rutlish School. The Institution initially leased the Church House property as additional trial grounds before later purchasing it. A stone urn which had once ornamented a gatepost to that house can be seen here on the left. Beyond are the chestnuts of Mostyn Road, and in the distance the poplars of Poplar Road.

36 Nelson Hospital. The South Wimbledon, Merton and District Cottage Hospital opened in 1900, at 173 Merton Road, Wimbledon, with six beds and two cots. It was soon realised, however, that larger purpose-built premises were needed and the centenary of Nelson's death gave the inspiration and incentive for a new district hospital to be built at The Rush. It was opened in 1912 and was enlarged by the War Memorial Wing in 1922, and later by a Maternity Wing in 1931. This view shows the original buildings, the middle one later being altered and enlarged. Note the private entrance on the right, and the hedge, later replaced with a wall.

37 The operating theatre at Nelson Hospital. Before the National Health Service Act of 1948 the hospital was financed by patients' fees and public donations. Fund-raising events were well supported; for many years an annual cricket match, organised by the great Surrey batsman, Jack Hobbs, raised funds for both the Nelson and the Wimbledon Cottage Hospital. Maurice Tate, 'Patsy' Hendren and Alf Gover were among the famous players seen on the local cricket ground. A well-funded and equipped hospital, the Nelson gained a good reputation for treatment and as a training establishment.

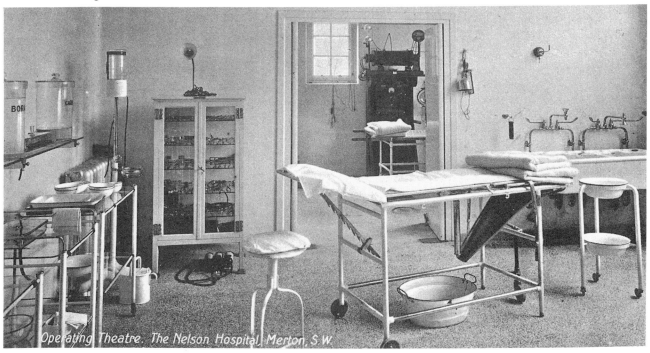

Operating Theatre. The Nelson Hospital, Merton, S.W.

MERTON PARK ESTATE
NORTH MORDEN, SURREY

Situated in an excellent position, in close proximity to the New Station on the C.&S.L. Tube Railway, from which there is a frequent and quick service to the City. Also within easy reach of the main Epsom Road, along which there is a Motor Bus Route.

Particulars of the Well-Built Residences (Some with spaces for Garages)

EDWIN EVANS & SONS,
Surveyors and Estate Agents,

146 Kingston Road, Merton Park, S.W.19

(on Estate)

Telephone : WIMBLEDON 1214

And at Clapham Junction, S.W.11

Telephone : BATTERSEA 0050 (Private Branch Exchange)

MESSRS. THOROGOOD, BROS. & SON

Builders,

(on Works) and at

36 Upper Brighton Road, Surbiton, Surrey

Solicitors :

HASLEWOOD, HARE & CO.,

139 Temple Chambers, Temple Avenue, E.C.4.

Telephone : CITY 0777

38 'Merton Park Estate' brochure, *c.*1928. Messrs. Thorogood built these houses in Sandbourne Avenue, which developed rapidly following the opening of the Underground extension.

39 Poplar Road South and Crown Lane. A view of *c.*1925 when the southern end of Poplar Road had begun to be developed following the sale by the Merton Park Estate Company of former allotment land on both sides of the road. 'North's Cottages' on the far side of Crown Lane had been built earlier by Thomas North of North Lodge, London Road, whose sheet-metal works in Southwark and Morden produced iron churches, houses and roofs on a large scale. These cottages were clad with corrugated iron. On the near side are some of the 19 dwellings designed by Quartermain in the late 1890s for John Innes's brickfield workers.

40 Although Circle Gardens was laid out by John Innes in the 1870s as part of his road plans, it was not until the late 1920s that it began to be developed. The early idea of a church in the centre was abandoned, and in 1928, when the council declined to purchase the circle as an open space, the houses in the middle were built, with tapering back gardens. By the date of this view, *c.*1931, R. Bilham & Sons had completed the outer ring of houses. The council resisted applications by the developer to build shops in or near the circle, or on corner sites on internal estate roads. The view is from Kenley Road north-west towards Poplar Road.

41 Marina Avenue, *c.*1935. The road, which gives access to the Sir Joseph Hood Recreation Ground, was originally called Recreation Road, but in September 1934 the name was changed to Marina Avenue, no doubt to mark the imminent marriage of the third son of George V to Princess Marina of Greece. The houses here are similar to some in Claremont Avenue, also built by Sidney Edward Parkes of Modern Homes & Estates. The West Barnes Lane shops visible in the background date from *c.*1926.

42 The new residents of Muchelney Road on the St Helier Estate can be seen standing outside their new homes in September 1931. Facing them is the pleasant open space of Moreton Green, which was often used for outdoor events and celebrations. There was a bird sanctuary here too, enclosed by rather dangerous iron railings, which were not regretted when removed for wartime salvage.

43 Torrington Way, Morden, was developed in 1932 and benefited from the Wimbledon to Sutton railway connection of 1930. The road was originally intended to continue on to Green Lane. In the field beyond, which survived until after the war, blackcurrant bushes were grown for many years.

TORRINGTON WAY
MORDEN. SURREY   14.

44 St Helier Avenue, looking north, *c*.1937. Alderman Lady St Helier of the LCC, who had striven for improved housing for Londoners, died in 1931 before the estate named after her was completed. This northern extension of the 1926 Sutton Bypass became the spine of the new estate and, by way of provision for the expected increase in use, the Avenue was widened to 33 metres (110 feet), with footpaths, cycle lanes and grass verges. Traffic lights were introduced at the Middleton Road junction, which had previously been marked by a long island, a hazard for buses making the turn. Mercury vapour lamps were installed here in 1938.

45 Crown House, *c*.1965. This huge development by Bernard Sunley & Sons, in the centre of Morden, was completed in 1961. A new *Crown*, with street-level bars and an upstairs function room, was built on the old village hall site, and when that was completed the old *Crown* was demolished and replaced by a Cater Brothers supermarket. In the centre of the island site stood 14 floors of office space.

46 The outlook from Crown House in 1961 with Morden Court in the bottom right-hand corner, and Rose Hill in the distance. In the foreground is a remnant of the land once given by Gilliat Hatfeild for Morden's first recreation ground. Most of it was acquired by the Underground for the railway extension and sheds, and the road frontage was sold for shops. The footbridge on the right was reluctantly built by the Underground to replace a length of the old footpath to Central Road. A car park has since replaced the poplar trees in the foreground.

47 The Morden Odeon, the ornamental 'island' and the BP garage dominate the foreground of this view looking eastward. All have now disappeared. In the distance the Phipps Bridge flats are under construction, and in between lies Morden Hall Park, which would lose many of those trees during the storms of 1987 and 1990.

48 The office development at Morden Station was under construction when this photograph was taken and was hardly an improvement to Charles Holden's austere design of 1926. The Co-op of 1940 was still on the site which would be redeveloped as offices and a street-level supermarket. Hawes furnishing store and Carsberg's carpets still occupied sites in Abbotsbury Road.

49 Windermere Avenue cuts across the left-hand corner of this photograph, and Kenley Road crosses near the middle. In the right-hand corner are the platforms of Morden station. The entrance to the tunnel can be seen, where the line goes beneath Kendor Gardens, visible beyond. The gardens take their name from Kenley and Dorset Roads. Against the trees of Morden Hall Park the tower of Jarvis's Morris House in Morden Road stands out. This striking 'temple of motoring' was demolished in 1987 when just 50 years old. In the distance are the three chimneys of the New Merton Board Mills. The Wimbledon-Croydon railway line cuts across between the industrial estates and the park.

Church and Chapel

The parish churches of St Mary the Virgin in Merton and St Lawrence in Morden were for centuries the only places for worship, and almost everyone went to church as a matter of course. The church married them, baptised their children, and buried them. Parish news was exchanged and parish decisions made beneath its roof.

The church at Morden was served by rectors from at least 1205 until 1301, when the parish was appropriated by Westminster Abbey, who owned the manor of Morden. The rectory was restored in 1634 by the Garth family, who purchased the manor after the Dissolution. During the lifetime of Merton Priory its canons would have been entrusted with the spiritual care of Merton parish. Later the poorly endowed living was a perpetual curacy in the gift of its lay rectors. Not until the mid-19th century was the incumbent designated 'vicar'.

A new parish, St Saviour's, Raynes Park, was created in 1907, and Holy Cross Mission Room was built in 1908 for a congregation which had till then been meeting in a room at the Seaforth Avenue post office. St John the Divine in High Path was consecrated in 1914, and for the Whatley estate St James's hall in Martin Way opened in 1934.

In Morden there was a mission church for a while in a converted stable in Wandle Road belonging to Colonel Bidder of Ravensbury Manor House, from which the new parish of St Peter took over in the early 1930s. St George's in Central Road opened as a hall in 1932, with a wooden church added in 1938. The rôles of these two buildings were later reversed. Emmanuel in Stonecot Hill and St Martin in Camborne Road came after the last war.

By 1725 there was a handful of Quakers and Presbyterians recorded in Merton, and Henry Meriton had licensed his own house as a Baptist meeting-place. It stood opposite the parish church, and Meriton was the lay rector at the time! In 1797 a preacher from Clapham began to hold open-air meetings in Merton, and rented a room in one of the Rush cottages. The whole house was later taken over, and in 1818 the group was constituted Merton Congregational Church. In 1841 it moved to a new chapel in Morden Road. Not until 1932 did Morden have a Congregational Church.

In 1885 a group from Wimbledon's Baptist congregation took an empty shop in London Road near the old *Crown* and began to attract members. Eleven years later the first sermon was preached in their new iron chapel (the 'Tin Tab') at the corner of Crown Road and Crown Lane. A school hall was opened in 1929 diagonally across the road, and now Morden Baptist Church occupies large premises which incorporate that hall. Another Baptist chapel was built in Botsford Road as part of the Whatley estate, and in 1960 Morden Park Baptist Chapel opened in Lower Morden Lane.

The Methodists were represented by a chapel in the High Street in the 19th century, and in 1934 they opened a hall in Martin Way, where a church was built in 1958. On the St Helier estate they built a church and large hall in Green Lane. The Salvation Army opened a citadel in Kingston Road in 1887, with later halls in Crown Lane and

Raynes Park. Scattered non-denominational mission rooms and evangelical chapels provided further spiritual and social support.

St Teresa, Bishopsford Road, was the district's first Roman Catholic church. As the Holy Family church and school it opened in 1931, and was soon strengthened by St Joseph's convent which opened nearby in Pollard Road. St John Fisher in Cannon Hill Lane began as a 'mass centre' in 1938, and the hall of Sacred Heart School in Burlington Road was used for a time by worshippers in western Merton.

50 St Mary the Virgin, *c*.1900. Merton's ancient parish church was built *c*.1115 by Gilbert the Norman, founder of Merton Priory, in the form of a long narrow nave and a small, probably apsidal, chancel. It is still a notably long narrow church, but it has been much altered, enlarged and improved, according to the tastes and needs of succeeding generations. The yew still survives, but the row of limes inside the churchyard wall fell victim to the 1987 storm. The tree in the road was removed in the improvements of 1911, which included the railed-off plantation in front of the church. By 1921 there was a lamp-post, a fire alarm and a telegraph post at this corner, all of which had to be moved elsewhere before the erection of the war memorial.

51 The interior of St Mary's. The early 18th-century west gallery, a gift of customs official William Baynes, was considered old-fashioned and inconvenient when this picture was taken in 1897. To mark Queen Victoria's Diamond Jubilee John Innes paid for its removal, as part of a scheme to open up the west end of the church. The 30 seats were replaced by 50 at the base of the tower. More light was admitted by means of new windows in the tower. The three old bells were rehung, and two new ones, one given by Innes and one by 'the ladies of the parish', were added. The funeral hatchment seen on the right is one of six, including those of Nelson, Sir William Hamilton and Rear Admiral Isaac Smith of Merton Abbey.

52 St Lawrence, Morden. St Lawrence is the only Grade I listed building in the locality. It is possible that there was a late Saxon church on this site, and there is known to have been one here, probably built of stone, in 1205. Little is then known of its history until the refurbishment completed in 1636, when the building was refaced with brick, the windows re-inserted, and a new brick tower built on the old footings and foundations. After the addition of a vestry in 1805 St Lawrence saw no more development until in 1983 a wing was added, with flexible space and facilities for meetings and other parish uses. This photograph of *c.*1875 shows the north side of the church. Beyond it on the left is the house, now known as the Manor House and much extended, which may have been built as a bailiff's house late in the 18th century as part of John Ewart's Morden Park estate.

53 A 'Christmas Greeting' view St Lawrence interior, *c.*1900. The pulpit of 1720 used to be a three-decker, and still has its sounding board. Once it stood to the west of this position; to resite it some of the monuments on the north wall had to be moved, and a small window had to be blocked up on the inside. The pulpit and the communion rail of the same date were gifts of Elizabeth Gardiner, who endowed the village school. The old box-pews with their folding brass candle-brackets were removed early in the 20th century. The upper tracery in the east window was designed in 1828 by parishioner Mrs. Mary Chambers.

54 St Mary's mission hall, Pincott Road. St Mary's church established a mission in the eastern part of Merton parish, initially in the Abbey Road schoolroom, and then, by 1887, in this mission hall in Pincott Road. Meetings, concerts and parties were held here, as well as worship. When the daughter church of St John the Divine opened in High Path in 1914, this building became St John's parish hall. As part of the rebuilding of the locality after the Second World War it was replaced by the present hall in High Path.

55 The parochial hall, Grand Drive. This building served as a church from 1902 until St Saviour's was built, and was then used as a parish hall until its demolition as part of the church extension in the early 1980s. In 1903 the iron building on the right replaced a smaller one which had been used for two years as the first church.

56 Grand Drive, 1911. The first vicar of St Saviour's, Rev. W.A. Birkbeck, was appointed in 1900. His father-in-law, hop merchant Sir Frederick Wigan, gave £2,000 towards building the church, which was completed in 1907. In this view looking north it is still surrounded by open fields and it remained relatively isolated until *c.*1924.

57 The Hope Mission was active from at least the end of the 19th century. By 1934 it had moved to Nelson Grove Road, where it has become Merton Evangelical Church, and this building in the High Street, seen here *c*.1970, was taken over by the undertaker's business next door for the manufacture and storage of coffins. It was pulled down in the redevelopment of the 1970s.

58 Merton Congregational chapel, 1953. The chapel in Morden Road, which had its own burial ground, was opened in 1841. A hall behind was used for the Sunday school and for the P.S.A. (Pleasant Sunday Afternoon) programme. Air-raid damage in 1940 closed the chapel, and a year later the hall was opened as a British Restaurant. Demand from local factory workers was so great that the chapel was repaired and equipped as an extension, and as part of a national promotion of British Restaurants a set of murals, designed by John Piper and painted on canvas by students at the Slade, were installed. This photograph was taken just before demolition in 1953 to make way for the High Path redevelopment; about 30 sets of human remains were exhumed for re-burial at Merton and Morden cemetery. The paintings were taken down when the restaurant closed and, it is believed, burnt.

59 St Mary's Sunday School party, 1954. Teachers and pupils pose in the old 'tin hut'. Until 1917 St Mary's had no church hall, and used a room in the old (and crumbling) Church House opposite or at the National Schools close by. So the opportunity was seized to acquire for £80 a dismantled iron building at Belvedere, Kent, which was erected on the site of the present church hall car park. It served the parish until 1965, when the new hall was built.

60 Martin Way, July 1935. On the left is the hall of the future church of St James, Beaford Grove. In 1931 Canon Jagger of St Mary's used an old sports pavilion in a field off Cannon Hill Lane to hold informal services for the growing population in this part of the parish. Then a suitable corner site was acquired, the hall was built and the first service held here in 1934. In 1938 work was begun on a church, but wartime and later building restrictions delayed its completion and consecration until 1957.

61 Gospel Tabernacle seen here in 1957, was built in 1952 opposite the old Congregational chapel in Morden Road. It seems that its congregation may have used the other building briefly before it was demolished. This one survived, latterly as the Underground Evangelism Church, until *c*.1980. Holly and Box Cottages, to the left, had been built soon after Nelson's death in 1805, on part of his estate. All three buildings were pulled down in the early 1980s.

62 St John Fisher, the Roman Catholic Church in Cannon Hill Lane, seen here in 1984. It was built in 1962 for a parish created in 1949 to take in parts of both Merton and Morden, but whose first mass had been held in 1938. The site had been occupied by farm buildings until at least 1930. Schools were opened in Grand Drive, and also attached to the parish is the convent of the Daughters of Our Lady of the Sacred Heart in Mostyn Road. This drawing is taken from a publication produced to mark the consecration of the church after it had been newly re-ordered.

Transport

Until the turnpike Acts of the 18th century, the condition of even main routes made travel always uncomfortable and sometimes dangerous. Once tolls could be levied to repair and maintain the roads, connections became quicker and more reliable. In Merton double gates were installed at what is now South Wimbledon crossroads, barring the road to London and the road to Epsom. However, travel for any distance was expensive. Most people, if they journeyed at all, had to walk, or to hope for a lift from a carter. However by the 1820s Merton was served by four short-stage coaches a day to London from the *King's Head* in the High Street, and Morden by one from the *George*. Both villages were also served by traffic on the ancient highway of Stane Street to Epsom, Dorking, and beyond. There were local carriers who transported goods, and the district, being within 10 miles of London, benefited from the penny post service introduced by an Act of 1710. Not far away the Surrey Iron Railway, in the early 19th century, took bulky loads down the Wandle valley to Wandsworth.

The year 1838 saw the opening between Nine Elms and Woking Common of the London & Southampton Railway (renamed London & South Western two years later), with a station at Wimbledon within relatively easy reach of at least some Merton residents. But there were only five trains a day, even the second-class return fare to Nine Elms was a shilling (5p), and not for ten years was the line extended to a new terminus called Waterloo Station.

There was no station in Merton or Morden until the opening in 1855 of the Wimbledon & Croydon line. This locally promoted venture was soon run jointly by the South Western and the London Brighton & South Coast Railways but then leased wholly to the L.B. & S.C. The station then called Morden Station (now Morden Road) was in fact in Merton and quite remarkably remote from centres of population. In 1868 stations were opened at Merton Abbey and Lower Merton, on the new Tooting, Merton & Wimbledon Railway. Two years later a platform on the Croydon line was added at Lower Merton, whose name was changed in 1887 at John Innes's insistence to Merton Park.

After the opening in 1871 of Raynes Park Station there were no new stations in the district for more than fifty years, when the rapid development of outer London after the 1914-8 war brought sharply increased demand for public transport.

In 1922 the Underground applied to build both a Wimbledon to Sutton line and an extension of the City and South London Railway line from Clapham Common, with a junction at Morden. The new Southern Railway objected strongly, and an agreement was reached which allowed the C. & S.L.R. its extension, but no junction, and authorised the Southern to build the Sutton line. It must be said that the C. & S.L.R. (which became the Northern Line in 1937) had the best of the deal. In its first week of operation in September 1926 it carried more than 300,000 passengers. To build South Wimbledon Station (the Underground chose this inaccurate name) the C. & S.L.R. had to rehouse 20 families whose homes were demolished. By contrast the new Morden Station was surrounded by farm fields.

Although the Sutton line had received Royal Assent in 1910 it was July 1929 before Wimbledon Chase (another misleading name) and South Merton stations opened. Morden South and St Helier followed in January 1930. Construction and compensation costs made the line expensive to build, and it has never been a real success. From the beginning it suffered from the proximity of the Underground with its feeder buses, and offered only a relatively slow service to the City.

At Merton Abbey Station the goods business expanded in the 1920s, with private sidings serving local factories, but competition from the Underground led to permanent closure of the passenger service in 1929.

Trams came to Merton in 1907, and motor buses in 1910. Morden had buses only along the Epsom and London Roads until the development of a busy terminus at the Underground station from 1926, when routes rapidly spread into Surrey, to Banstead, Wallington, Sutton, Worcester Park, and Epsom.

With the increased road traffic as the 20th century developed the old roads had to be repeatedly resurfaced, widened and straightened. New 'arterial' roads to bypass Sutton and Kingston were constructed in the 1920s, with local connecting roads, the future St Helier Avenue, and Bushey Road.

63 Raynes Park station, *c.*1900, was opened in 1871 to serve an estate which was planned to be built south of the Epsom branch of the London & South Western Railway by Morden's Richard Garth. For his development Garth had already chosen the name Raynes Park, which commemorated the Rayne family, formerly owners of West Barnes Farm.

The station layout was altered in 1884; this view shows the line to Epsom, on the southern side of the station. The mainline tracks are out of sight on the left, while the up line from Epsom goes underneath and is served by a platform on the north side.

64 Merton Park level crossing, *c*.1900. Almost from the first a source of complaint, the level crossing in Kingston Road, now an 'A' road, has nevertheless survived. In this view the signal box is of the old LBSCR elevated type; a replacement at ground level was installed late in 1913. The *White Hart*, close by, still offered 'Livery & Bait Stables', as well as 'Billiards & Bowling Green'. The four Leigh Villas, on the right, still survive, but Boyne Lodge (formerly Darmstadt House), behind the trees, was replaced by the telephone exchange in 1931. In the distance is Spring House, pulled down in 1935.

65 Merton Park footbridge, *c*.1907. In 1896, south of the station, the LBSCR built this unusually long footbridge which allowed a safe crossing of both the Croydon and Tooting lines and became a local landmark. The railway company insisted on wicket gates at the bottom of the steps to keep sheep and cattle from straying onto them. Today only the crossover at the Dorset Road end survives. In the distance some of the houses of Branksome, Bournemouth and Melbourne Roads on the 'station estate' can be seen. These were built in 1906-7.

66 The London General Omnibus Company garage. The Merton High Street garage, built in November 1913, was one of five opened in that year (two had opened in 1912) to cater for the suburban expansion of bus services. We can see that this is a summer scene—the boys are paddling in the Wandle and the three drivers are in their summer uniform of white coats and caps. In front of the garage run the tramlines of the London United Tramways Company.

67 The West Barnes crossing, *c.*1907-14. Looking eastward from Burlington Road with its tramlines, on the left is the entrance lodge to the Blue House Farm estate of Charles Blake. Beyond the trees of Pyl Brook there seem to be sheep grazing on Raynes Park golf course, once Edward Rayne's farm. On the right is West Barnes Terrace of *c.*1884, built by Blake, behind which are the shops of Seaforth Avenue, developed in the early years of the 20th century by W.F. Palmer of the nearby Blagdon's Farm.

West Barnes, Crossing.

68 Burlington Road, 1911. Development in this road, laid out in the 1870s, was slow, mainly because of drainage problems. Cavendish and Belmont Avenues, which began to be developed in 1905, can be seen on the right. On the left freehold land in New Malden is advertised. The tram tracks were laid in 1907 by London United, whose trams from Kingston and New Malden reached Wimbledon via Worple Road and continued along Broadway and Merton High Street to the then Surrey/LCC border at Tooting.

69 'Merton Tramways Junction' between 1906 and 1913. Not strictly a junction at all—the traveller from Merton to London had to change trams here at the Surrey/LCC border, where Colliers Wood and Tooting meet. On the left is a LUT 1902 car which had come from Hampton Court, and on the right a Class E LCC car from Blackfriars. While the LUT trams used the overhead current, those of the LCC used conduits in the road. In the early 1920s the tracks were connected.

70 Croft Road, 1912. On 5 December 1912 LGOC route 48 from Tottenham was extended from Stockwell to the *Nelson Arms*, Merton. This was the district's first motor bus service. Every four minutes between 7.15 a.m. and 11.15 p.m. the buses turned round by using Abbey Road/Croft Road/Mill Road. The picture shows what Croft Road (laid out in 1905) looked like after 14 days, its surface of rammed flints battered by the solid tyres of the B type buses. After a brief trial of the *Grove* as terminus, Croft Road was again used, but only for reversing into for turning. Then in May 1913 the route was extended to the *Duke of Edinburgh* in Kingston Road, at the corner of Southey Road. And in January 1914 it was extended again, to Raynes Park. Croft Road was left in peace.

71 The flooded claypits at the old brickfield in Green Lane, Merton, which had long been an illicit playground for the boys of the district, became one of the sites used for dumping spoil from the excavation for the Underground extension. The overhead carrier which can be seen against the sky ran behind the buildings in London Road and Crown Lane and over Poplar Road. The site was later landscaped and opened as Mostyn Gardens in 1936.

72 Platform construction at Morden station, February 1926. The two Victorian villas, Heathfield and Sunnyside, on the south side of London Road, survived into the 1930s, to be replaced by shops. On the far right is the *Crown*.

73 Morden station garage, *c*.1926. To encourage motorists to use the new service the Underground authority provided parking under cover for more than 300 cars and 200 bicycles and motorbikes. Petrol, car-cleaning and light repairs were available. Theatre-goers from further out in Surrey as well as businessmen were among the patrons.

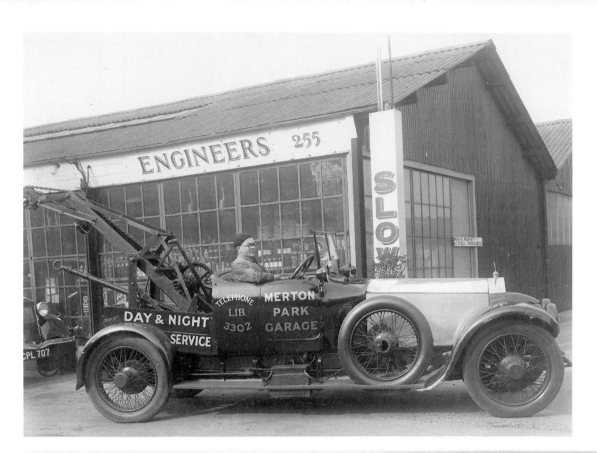

74 Merton Park garage, 1934. Architect Sydney Brocklesby, who had his home and office at Long Lodge in Kingston Road, opened this garage in part of his grounds in 1926, seeing a promise of good business derived from the opening of the Kingston Bypass. The Rolls Royce breakdown vehicle, with its powerful lifting-gear, suggests that the venture did indeed prosper.

75 Morden station, March 1936. A view taken from the cinema projectionist's escape balcony. Buses old and new are serving the queues of travellers from town. By this date development of the one-time farm fields of southern Merton Park was complete.

76 A view showing traffic to Epsom in 1928, from the station canopy. Extra buses were brought in from elsewhere during Epsom week, when crowds like this were seen every day at Morden. One of Morden Hall's lodge cottages can be seen in the distance, and the south side of London Road is still bordered by fields and grand old trees. Edwin Evans, the estate agents, moved from their offices at 146 Kingston Road to The Parade, Morden (later numbered 64 London Road) at the end of 1927. The move reflected the shift in development resulting from the Underground extension. Though the firm has long since left Morden, its name can still be seen today at the back of this building.

77 Merton High Street, 6 January 1951. An E1 class car, originally run by the LCC and dating from 1922, is seen here on the last day of service. Most of the E1 cars, which were designed for speed, were based at Clapham. At the left of the picture can be seen the indicator that told the driver if the length of single track around the corner in Merton Road was clear.

78 London Road, *c.*1949, and of the six buses in this view four are wartime utility Daimlers. The bus on the left, which is on route 127, is specially low-built, to negotiate the bridge at Worcester Park. Third from the right is a Bristol, borrowed from the provinces.

79 Kingston Road, *c.*1950. A wartime utility Daimler bus on route 152 approaches the level crossing. These Daimlers were used only at Merton and Sutton garages. The signal box, erected in 1913, survived until 1984 when it was replaced by automatic gates. An 'essential repairs' certificate was issued in 1945 for the war-damaged *White Hart*, but it was not rebuilt until the 1950s. The long roof beyond the *White Hart* is Rutlish School.

80 Wimbledon-Sutton railway bridge, London Road, 1930. This photograph from *The Railway Engineer* gives a deck view of the steel lattice girder bridge over London Road, Morden, which was constructed by the Horsley Bridge & Engineering Company of Tipton. In the background is the island platform of Morden South Station, which like South Merton Station was built with provision for future street-level buildings, which did not materialise. Wimbledon Chase and St Helier Stations are more elaborate.

Education

The first school in the area must have been the one at Merton Priory, where the sons of noble or ambitious families came to be educated in the Middle Ages. Otherwise the earliest school known here was the one in Central Road, Morden, founded in 1731 for poor children of the parish, which opened with 12 pupils. In 1878, when there were more than 100, it became a National school. Despite improvements the building was condemned as small and insanitary, and in 1910 Surrey County Council built a new school in London Road. Morden also had a Sunday school from an early date. Dr. Peers, rector at the time, founded it in 1791 and built the church gallery to accommodate the children.

Merton's National School opened *c.*1830, on the east side of Church Lane. Built with funds raised locally and a grant from the National School Society, it struggled against the apathy of subscribers, and the drift of the children to local factories. Richard Thornton's bequest of 1865 enabled the parish to build new schools—for boys, girls and infants—a little to the south of the old school, which was demolished. Abbey Road Infants School served the east of the parish from 1836.

Most children completed their education at the National schools.

However in 1892 a cookery school funded by the Rutlish Charity had opened in Kingston Road for 'Ladies, Servants, and Young Women', and was attended by many girls of school age. From 1895 Rutlish Science School gave able boys the chance to continue beyond elementary schooling, and a pupil-teacher centre at the Gladstone Road Technical Institute opened in 1905, and developed into Wimbledon County School for Girls, though not till 1924.

By the early 20th century western Merton was developing fast. In 1906 a temporary school opened in Aston Road, and three years later Merton Urban District Council built large new schools in Botsford Road. Education reforms and population growth brought replacement schools for younger children at Merton Abbey and Merton Park in the 1920s and new schools for newer areas in the 1930s. A Roman Catholic school was built in Burlington Road, and Raynes Park County School for boys opened in 1936.

The development of the LCC St Helier Estate brought an urgent need for large new schools. By 1931 two had opened on either side of St Helier Avenue. Each consisted of a mixed infant department and a single-sex upper department, and until after the last war each was known simply as School No. 1, 2, 3 or 4. In Montacute Road the St Helier Roman Catholic School, later St Teresa's, was built.

Since the war, while some new schools have appeared in Merton and Morden, demographic changes as well as new education policies have also brought closure or altered usage.

Private education would once have been at home, perhaps with tutors or governesses, though many older boys and some girls went away to school. Before the end of the 18th century Miss Rutter's Boarding School in Morden offered instruction in English, French and needlework; and a Mr. Rutter nearby was proprietor of Mordon (an old spelling) House Academy. For much of the next century the Whites at Morden Hall and the de Chastelains at Church House, Merton, catered for the sons of the middle classes by providing grammar, arithmetic, French, a few 'extras', plain food and country air.

Private day schools proliferated from the late 19th century, although few survived the last war. In Merton Park were Miss Godwin's School for Ladies in Dorset Road from 1888-96; Fairlawn School, started by Rose Brocklesby in 1895; Blakesley House School, next to the Nelson Hospital from 1913-39; Cranmore College at 164 Kingston Road from 1923; and Birnam School in Church Lane from 1931 until bombed out, when it moved to Merton Hall Road, returning to rebuilt premises after the war. In Grand Drive were Cumberland House (1924) and Kingsley High School (1927), as well as St David's School, which had opened in Holy Cross hall off West Barnes Lane in the 1920s and survived until c.1970.

Night school classes were held at the Merton Schools by 1868, taught by the headmaster. Later venues included the cookery school, Rutlish School, the Manor Club, Morden's Village Club, and the Gladstone Road Institute.

81 The old schoolhouse, Morden. In 1719 Mrs. Elizabeth Gardiner, daughter of George Garth, died and left £300 to provide free schooling according to the Church of England for poor children of the parish. A piece of land in Central Road (then Morden Lane) was leased at a peppercorn rent from Richard Garth IV, and the school opened in 1731. It was enlarged in 1872 and an infants' room added in 1889, giving a capacity of 190 children. In 1910 the building became the parish hall. A large plaque commemorates Mrs. Gardiner and her gift to the parish. The porch seen here was removed c.1930 at the insistence of the LCC, which had purchased the land right up to that point.

82 Morden Hall Academy was founded by Rev. John White *c*.1830 and run by his son Thomas from the early 1840s until it closed *c*.1870. Here some of the pupils are playing cricket on the lawn to the north of the building. The large extension is shown on the left and the bell turret is just visible. Some numbers of the *Mordonian Gazette*, the school newspaper, survive, which give a picture of school life here. Mr. and Mrs. White seem to have given the boys a happy enough time, with plenty of fresh air.

83 A view of Morden Hall, probably from the 1830s, showing the south front. The bell in the turret, generally assumed to date from when the hall was used as a school, had been installed. This view shows the main gates and what is perhaps a free interpretation of the landscaping. The colonnade which connected the wings of the house in earlier years has gone. [Manning and Bray, *History of Surrey* (extra-illustrated), British Library shelf-mark: Crach.1.Tab.1.b.1.]

84 The Merton Church Schools, 1919. When Richard Thornton of Cannon Hill, a marine insurance millionaire, died in 1865 he left £10,000 to endow schools for the parish, for boys, girls and infants. The new building went up on a site facing the churchyard and was opened in 1870 by the Bishop of Winchester. The schools grew rapidly and the building was enlarged several times. In 1926 a new infants' school was built nearby and the old building became a Central School. It ended its days as a mixed Church of England secondary school in the 1960s, and was used as a special school and adult evening centre before the building was sold. The newer extensions were demolished for a development of retirement flats, and the range seen here was converted into apartments.

MERTON SCHOOLS.

Programme of

ENTERTAINMENT

at the

MISSION HALL,

Thursday Evening, May 10th, 1894,

To commence at 7.45. o'clock,

Conductor: *MR. PILLINGER.*

The proceeds, after payment of expenses, to be
devoted to the Abbey Road School Fund.

85 School concert programme, 1894. The Abbey Road Infants School, built *c*.1836, was a parish school, but the condition of its building was so bad that it was threatened with losing its grant and being taken over by Surrey Education Committee as a Board school. Throughout 1894 fund-raising events were held in Merton to raise the £450 needed for improvements. This was the cover for a concert programme performed by the children of the Merton Schools at the Mission Hall in Pincott Road. So successful was it that a second performance was given at the Drill Hall in St George's Road, Wimbledon. Mr. Pillinger was for 37 years headmaster of the boys' school and choirmaster and organist at St Mary's.

86 Merton Abbey Primary School, *c*.1970. Accommodation at the old Abbey Road Infants School remained barely adequate. For years the local council pressed the County Council to provide a replacement. The First World War was only one cause for the delay, and it was not until 1927 that a new school opened, in this attractive building in High Path.

87 Rutlish Science School, 1895. When William Rutlish, Court Embroiderer to Charles II and a native of Merton, died in 1687 he left the income from his Merton properties to pay for apprenticeships for poor boys and girls of the parish. Two hundred years later the funds had increased hugely, as had Merton's population, but the demand for apprenticeships was tiny. After several years of debate a scheme to use some of the money to build a boys' school for Merton and Wimbledon was approved by the Charity Commissioners. John Innes was the principal mover, and his estate architect, H.G. Quartermain, designed the building, which opened in September 1895 in Kingston Road, on the site of some of the tenement properties bequeathed by William Rutlish. The building which cost £6,500 is seen here nearing completion. It was pulled down early in the 1970s.

88 Rutlish School art room, *c.*1925. Despite the original name of the school—'science schools' were the thing to provide for boys at the time— Rutlish offered from the start a wide curriculum: English grammar, composition and literature, the usual branches of mathematics, French, German, geography, English history, 'vocal music', drill, shorthand, woodwork, drawing, and more. Very soon after the school opened adult education classes began to be held here, too.

89 Morden Council School. The small endowed school in Central Road had become too cramped by the start of the 20th century. In March 1910 the Surrey County Council replaced it with the Council School, in London Road, which could accommodate 300 children. Joseph Henry Rewcastle was headmaster and Mrs. Rewcastle was headmistress of the infants' department. They had been in charge of the old school from *c*.1895, and were known for their strictness. Between 1901 and 1931 Mr. Rewcastle also served first as clerk and assistant overseer to Morden Parish Council and then as rate collector for Morden.

90 Raynes Park Schools, October 1913. These schools were built by the new Merton Urban District Council in 1909, for 350 boys, 350 girls and 340 infants. A building for special subjects (housecraft, woodwork and metalwork) was added two years later. The only road access then was by the unmade Botsford Road, and the schools were generally known as the Botsford Road Schools. They are seen here from what is now Cannon Hill Common, the foreground now being part of the Joseph Hood Recreation Ground. The buildings survive (though the little belvedere has gone) as Merton Adult College, and the Joseph Hood First School.

91 Blakesley House, 1978. There was a building here by 1865, and as plain Blakesley it was the home of Patrick Edwardes, brother of George Edwardes of Daly's Theatre, before becoming Blakesley House School in 1913. Jack and Alice Dudley, who had met and married as members of staff at Merton Boys' School, were the proprietors and principal teachers. It was a preparatory school for boys and girls, who wore green blazers edged with gold braid, and matching caps or berets. Later it had a senior boys' department. The school moved to Worcester Park in 1939 when this building was requisitioned as a wartime first-aid post. In 1943 it was acquired by the Nelson Hospital, and housed the physiotherapy department until pulled down in 1985. Its name survives in Blakesley Walk, the old right of way known until 1925 as Blind Lane.

92 Poplar Road School infants, 1935. The southern part of Merton developed rapidly after the Underground extension of 1926, and not before time Poplar Road School was opened in May 1932. In their rather stark classroom, with its long desks, 42 infants posed with their teacher.

93 Manor House Nursery School, *c*.1950. John Innes's Manor House in Watery Lane, which under his will passed to the John Innes Horticultural Institution, was taken over as a wartime day nursery in 1943. After the war the council decided to continue the provision, but as a nursery school. As such it remained here until Rutlish School moved to the site in 1957. The nursery school then transferred to a pair of large semi-detached houses in Kingston Road, Lakefield and Thorndale, which had been briefly occupied by a temporary junior school, called Merton Rush School.

Employment

For centuries most work in Merton and Morden was agricultural. Away from the Wandle's old floodplain the soil is not particularly fertile, but wheat was grown, together with general produce, and there was pasture for cows and a few sheep.

Power for grinding the corn came from the Wandle. There was a mill already on the site chosen for Merton Priory early in the 12th century. The Amery mill, west of Merton bridge and south of the High Street, ground corn originally, and later dyewoods. It was a copper works before becoming a paper mill, the forerunner of Merton Board Mills. What was generally known as Merton corn mill was just over the border in Wimbledon parish; in its final years it became Connolly's leather works.

In Morden there was a paper mill just upstream from Mitcham Bridge, of which only the wheel pit survives. Snuff was also ground at this site, at Ravensbury Mill and at Morden Cottage.

Other industries grew up near the Wandle. James Jacob was a whitster or calico bleacher at Merton Abbey before 1700. His workers, men, women and children, walked all day up and down the bleaching grounds, scooping water over the spread lengths of cloth. Printing of calico and other fabrics was also carried out at Merton Abbey sites. It was somewhere here in the mid-18th century that Francis Nixon developed the use of engraved copper plates, rather than wood blocks, to produce designs of exquisite detail. Nearer our own time the names of Morris and Liberty would bring new fame for Merton designs.

As the 19th century proceeded, and Nelson's Merton Place estate was sold off for building, many small businesses sprang up—carpenters, saddlers, builders, even a gun and bicycle maker. A school admission book of 1868-74 lists a wide variety of fathers' occupations, including master dyer, plate polisher, fancy printer, snuff grinder, station master, photographer, india rubber worker, coachman, cowman, gravel digger and policeman.

Paul Addington's varnish works had opened near Phipps Bridge by 1860 and early in the 20th century another big employer arrived in eastern Merton. Foster & Co., an arc lamp works set up in 1903 by Milton Ely of the Wimbledon department store family, moved to a large site at The Path, west of Morden Road.

The District Council designated three factory zones. East of Morden Road came Lines Brothers' toy factory and Dean's Rag Book Co. To Burlington Road came Bradbury & Wilkinson, security printers, to West Barnes Lane Carters Tested Seeds and to Bushey Road British Salmson Aero Engines and Senior's fishpaste factory. Somewhat later Garth Road's slaughterhouse and tallow works were replaced by electrical, instrument, joinery and light engineering works.

These three areas expanded and still exist today as centres of employment, but now their strengths are less in manufacture than in retailing and administration, and many jobs have been lost within Merton and Morden.

94 'A View at Merton Abbey'. This undated scene almost certainly represents the Merton Abbey print works (now Merton Abbey Mills). The large house in the background seems to be Abbey House, once part of the Priory, but much altered, which was demolished in 1914. However the wheelhouse shown looks quite different from the present one on the site.

95 Ploughing at Morden Hall Farm. The farm was once part of the Garth family holdings, but when John Innes arrived in Merton in 1865 it became one of his early purchases. It occupied land west of Morden Road and north of London Road and Crown Lane, and was a mixed farm, but mainly dairy. The trees in the background may be those of Morden Road.

96 Haystack making at Morden, *c*.1910. On Gilliat Hatfeild's estate his bailiff, Abraham Clark (the man in the cart), supervises the building of this large haystack, near the future site of Aberconway Road. A mechanical elevator hoists the hay, to be stacked by an assorted team of workers above. The completed stack would be roofed with the furled sheet of canvas, for weather protection.

97 Morden Hall Farm Dairy, *c.*1900. The milkmen with their carts pose in front of the main range of farm buildings, on the site of the present Mann Egerton garage. From 1866 the farm was managed for John Innes by members of the White family. Oscar James White ran his Morden Hall Farm Dairy from here for more than 30 years, until *c.*1920, with a number of shops in Merton, Wimbledon and even Tooting. In 1914 the farm occupied about 160 hectares (400 acres) and provided butter, cream, eggs and poultry, and Jersey and goat's milk as well as ordinary cow's milk. The dairy became part of United Dairies *c.*1926. The pastures were sold for housing and the farmhouse in Morden Road was pulled down in 1930, but the Kenley Road site continued as a bottling depot until the late 1980s.

98 Dairy roundsman, *c.*1910. Not all Oscar White's men used a horse-cart. Milk was delivered twice a day, and the roundsman had to clean all his equipment, including those cans (half-pint, pint and quart), and polish the brass trim on the churns and the cart. He then had to do his bookwork—most customers paid each day. In the background Merton Park's long footbridge can just be seen.

99 Broadwater Farm Dairy, 1913. At this date Broadwater, or Bakers End, Farm was in the tenancy of Mr. Berkshire. Under an earlier proprietor, Mr. Keevil, the dairy was the source of an outbreak of scarlet fever, and the process seen here, of straining milk through a cloth into a churn, does not look very hygienic—this was before the days of pasteurisation. The dairy was taken over by the Royal Arsenal Co-operative Society in 1939. It stood on the site of the present Co-op car-park; the other farm buildings had been replaced in 1923 by the cul-de-sac called Bakers End.

100 Ravensbury Mills. There was a mill here *c*.1680, but sited only on the Mitcham bank of the river. It is not known what was then ground here, but later there was logwood milling (for dyestuffs), and by the middle of the 18th century snuff was being milled here and the works had been enlarged to straddle the river. The buildings in this view date from the beginning of the 19th century, by which time the greater part of the works was sited on the Morden bank, where two wheels worked in parallel. In 1805 the Ravensbury mills were taken over by John Rutter, from a local family, who was established as a manufacturer of tobacco and snuff in the City. Rutters ran the works until 1925, increasingly producing pipe and cigarette tobacco as well as snuff. From 1925 to *c*.1980 Whitely Products Ltd. were here, making items such as cords, straps and the 'Whitely Exerciser' chest expander. At the time of writing the main mill buildings are being converted to residential use as part of a development of apartments, but it is intended that the Wandle Industrial Museum will also be housed here, and the wheels restored.

101 Morden Hall snuff mills, *c*.1939. This view dates from the last days of Morden Hall as a London Hospital annexe. The two breast-shot water wheels were here until 1968, when the one on the left was removed. The mill building on the left is thought to date from *c*.1830, and the one on the right (covered with ivy) is older. From 1760 the Polhill family leased the snuff mills from the Garths. They were followed by Taddy & Co. in 1845, and then by Alexander Hatfeild in 1854. The white timber building is the west wing of Morden Cottage, which Hatfeild made his home. His son Gilliat purchased the Garth lands and it was as lords of the manor that he and then his son continued the business until 1922, when Gilliat Edward Hatfeild closed it down in response to a strike at the London premises. He made his home here in Morden Cottage, though his father had preferred the Hall. On his death in 1941 the Morden Hall estate passed to the National Trust.

102 The Morris works, 1913. William Morris, poet, political thinker and designer, took over this site in 1881 from Welch's printing business, which used to produce what Morris called 'hideous red and green tablecloths'. He was attracted by the picturesque buildings, including ranges of tarred timber workshops and a good house fronting the High Street, by the mill-pond, water-meadows and gardens, and by the 'abundant and good' Wandle water. Here he concentrated on a limited number of lines. This large shed, just south of the High Street, housed the stained glass workshop. In other buildings were tapestry and carpet looms, textile looms, dye-vats and printing tables. Morris's friend, the potter William De Morgan, had tile-kilns close by for a few years.

103 Morris works, *c.*1936. Mr. Chadwick and his nephew Frank Chadwick were members of a local family with a tradition of employment at the Morris works, mainly as dyers. Here they are plunging lengths of cloth into the deep indigo vats that William Morris had installed 50 years before. After Morris's death in 1896 the works continued, from the late 1920s as Morris & Co. Art Workers Ltd. The buildings, some of which were already frail, suffered bomb damage in 1940 and the works closed soon afterwards. The site was taken over by the New Merton Board Mills, and is now occupied by flats and part of the Savacentre development.

104 Young & Co. showroom, 1929. In 1919 a company specialising in high-quality farm and country estate equipment built its showroom in High Path opposite Abbey Road. This illustration is taken from their catalogue of 1929, 'The Hygienic Housing of Livestock'. Note the label that says, 'BRITISH GOODS ARE BEST'! Young's were here until after the last war, but their building has now gone.

105 Bradbury & Wilkinson. In 1919 Merton and Morden Council, who were seeking 'high-class' factory developments for the western side of the district, were delighted to be approached by Bradbury & Wilkinson, banknote and security printers. The works opened in Burlington Road in 1921, and the £2,000 increase in the rates revenue was welcome, but the councillors had not reckoned with the huge amount of extra waste water, laden with paper pulp, that would flow into the drains! Bradbury's was one of Merton and Morden's biggest employers, until they left in the mid-1970s. Since 1987 the site has been occupied by a Tesco superstore.

106 Lines Bros. factory, *c.*1958. A big development in the Morden Road factory estate was Lines Bros. factory, which came in 1923, and was later enlarged. Their Pedigree and Tri-Ang products became known all over the world. During the last war Lines switched production to such diverse items as Sten guns and the metal components of suspenders, and also made models of German planes for aircraft recognition training. Here 21-inch walking dolls come down the conveyor belt to be inspected and boxed. A resident sculptor was employed to design 'fresh and lifelike' heads and bodies. The departure of the business in 1972 was a great shock, for Lines was one of the largest employers in the area, particularly of women.

107 Reed's Paper Mills, 1913. The Metropolitan Paper Co. was operating a paper mill at the old Merton Copper Mills site in the High Street by 1895. It was taken over in 1898 by Albert E. Reed, founder of Reed International, who already owned several other mills. On the right of the picture is a stretch of the Priory walls.

108 DRG Board Mills, 1982. What had once been Reed's paper mills became Merton Board Mills in 1923, in a large new factory. After being wound up in 1925 it re-emerged as New Merton Board Mills. In the Second World War this was where local residents brought waste paper for salvage. The works were bombed, but were rebuilt and enlarged, taking in the whole of the Morris & Co. site as well. Cardboard containers were made here, and in its last years this was the Merton Packaging Works of the Dickinson Robinson Group. It closed in the early 1980s and was demolished in 1985. Most of the site is now occupied by Savacentre.

109 Government Instructional Factory, 1924. Tomlin's mineral water works, which had been built in 1899 on the corner of Milner Road and Morden Road, became the Magnet Laundry by 1909. Then in 1920 a training works for local disabled ex-servicemen was established here, under a Ministry of Labour scheme. It was only a short-lived project, however; this view dates from an application by Jarvis & Sons to develop the site as a garage. They remained here until 1935 when they moved to much larger premises further down Morden Road.

110 'Mr. Littler's Factory', 1894. Edmund Littler came to Merton from Waltham Abbey in 1831 taking over two factories and other property, and developing as a printer of fine silks and wools. The Littler of the date of this view was another Edmund, probably a grandson of the original. Arthur Lasenby Liberty became Littler's best customer and ultimately bought the works in 1904. Edmund Littler continued to live nearby until 1909 when, becoming anxious about his affairs (needlessly, as he had a generous annuity from Liberty, as well a healthy rent-roll), he shot himself with his own pistol. The old Colour House can be seen in the background and to its right the New Shop (later Coles Shop). The timber buildings were probably more than 100 years old at this date.

111 Liberty works, 1963. With its neat lawns and creeper-covered buildings the Liberty works formed an unusually attractive group. Arthur Lasenby Liberty replaced some of the old buildings used by Littler's. Seen here are the Long Shop (extreme right) and the 1926 or Apprentice Shop (right of centre). The roof of what was known as the Loft (now called the Show House) can be seen behind the Colour House. All these buildings survive as part of the Merton Abbey Mills Market.

112 The Kandyan gate, 1945. Liberty's filled in one of the long ponds on its land on the left bank of the Wandle, and laid out a sports ground and tennis courts for its employees. Between the remaining ponds the 'Kandyan gate' was built. This was really a covered wooden bridge, decorated with exotic carving. Seen here are tier girls, Lily Clarke and Joan Allen. Tier girls (and boys) assisted the printers in the preparation and marking out of the cloth on the printing table and then in the application of the dyes. The site is now part of a factory estate.

113 'Made in Morden!', 1957. Walter Instruments was founded in 1926 and at the Garth Road works, which was set back on the south-west side of the road with a coffee-stall in front, they made fluorescent lights, radio components, domestic appliances (including the 'No-Cord' iron), and, from 1948, tape-recorders. The site is now occupied by a modern block. [illustration from *Merton and Morden Official Guide, c.1957,* pub. Ed. J. Burrow & Co. Ltd.]

114 Merton Park Studios, 1966. Part of Long Lodge was leased to Publicity Films Ltd. in 1934, while the rest of the premises was still occupied by the Brocklesby family. By 1939 the Brocklesbys had left and the whole building was taken over by Merton Park Studios Ltd. and associated companies. Training and propaganda films were made here during the war, and when peace came production turned to information, education and advertising films. Frederic Shields' studio was rebuilt and workshops were added. Many second feature films were made here, and an Edgar Lustgarten series, and its dubbing and recording facilities were used by other companies. In 1967 what had become the Film Producers' Guild ceased production in Merton Park, only the film library continuing to function; and in 1976 Long Lodge was sold. The grounds were developed for housing and the house has become a set of office suites, with a pleasant garden in front. In the development one of Brocklesby's charming flint cottages was demolished. This was Marlestan, which had been named for the original owner's children, Marjorie, Leslie and Stanley Peters, and had later served as a store for the studios.

115 The John Innes Horticultural Institution's Cytology Laboratory, 1937. The Institution was opened in 1910, in John Innes's Manor House grounds, under Dr. William Bateson FRS, Professor of Biology at Cambridge, and soon won a reputation for research in plant genetics and biology. Indeed it was Dr. Bateson who coined the word 'genetics'. At the right in this photograph is cytologist (cell scientist) C.D. Darlington, who was director from 1939-53. The Institition moved to a much larger site at Bayfordbury, near Hertford, after the last war, and in 1967 another move took it to the campus of the University of East Anglia in Norwich, where, as the John Innes Centre, it functions as a research and educational establishment of international importance.

CARTERS AT RAYNES PARK.

WHEEL FOR TESTING GRASSES AND GRASS MANURES.

116 Carters Tested Seeds was founded in 1837 in High Holborn by James Carter. In 1909 the firm bought eight hectares (19 acres) of land on the west side of West Barnes Lane and began to build this imposing complex of offices, laboratories and workshops. Carters was one of the largest employers in the district and the beautiful grounds were a landmark, especially for rail travellers, until in 1966 the business was bought by Cuthbert's Seeds and the site was sold. The council bought the land in 1967 for housing and laid out a number of roads with 'garden' names, commemorating Carters itself in the name of the central building. These views are from an undated Carters publication.

Leisure

We know that the country sports of hunting, shooting and fishing were enjoyed in Merton and Morden. There are accounts of fox-hunting and stag-hunting in the 19th century; tracts of western Merton were covered with water for several months each year, giving good sport for wild-fowlers; and the Wandle was once famous for its trout.

Cricket and football of course flourished. But by the beginning of the 20th century new forms of recreation had arrived. Cycling, golf, lawn tennis, amateur dramatics, poetry readings and music making were pursued by the more leisured residents. There were gardening societies and hiking groups; Merton's Manor Club and Morden's Village Club offered billiards and bowls, debates and 'smoking concerts'. Magic lantern slides drew crowds of all ages. In the High Street a roller skating rink opened in 1909, and on the opposite corner of Mill Road the Abbey Cinematograph opened a year later.

For children the country pleasures of field, pond and rickyard were varied with school and Sunday school treats, which might be a picnic and games, or a trip to the pantomime, Crystal Palace or Hampton Court, or even an excursion, by special train, to the seaside. Miss Hatfeild ran a boys' club in Morden, and John Innes founded one in Merton to provide 'wholesome' recreation.

After the first war there was a new craze for dancing. Classes in the foxtrot and tango, blackbottom and Charleston, opened; tennis and cricket clubs held 'flannel dances'. New recreation grounds made tennis and bowls available to everyone, and though local people had to wait until well after the next war for a swimming-pool there was one not too far away, in Wimbledon. Morden Cinema opened in 1932 and the Odeon at Shannon Corner in 1938. The wireless and the gramophone were new recreational pleasures of the period, and who could resist the thrill of motoring on the new arterial roads?

Today the pattern of leisure is different again. Tennis courts and bowling-greens are less used, and television and the VCR have closed the cinemas, but football and cricket still thrive, fitness trails and indoor sports halls have arrived, and people socialise in the pubs and restaurants.

117 The *White Hart* bowling-green, 1914. Behind the *White Hart* was for many years this green—a popular local facility. The 'long pavilion' in the picture was often used for dinners and local gatherings.

118 Manor Club and Masonic Hall, *c*.1900. John Innes was responsible for both these buildings. The architect H.G. Quartermain's drawing probably just predates the construction of the Masonic Hall, on the right. As built it shows a number of variations from this version. Merton Lodge, No. 2790, was unable to raise the £1,000 needed to purchase the hall after Innes's death in 1904 and had to vacate it. In 1943, after housing Merton and Morden Central Library, it became Merton Public Hall. The Manor Club, which dates from 1890, offered a reading-room, lectures, whist, billiards, bowls, allotments, cycling and rambling and a bar which served beer and cider—John Innes would not permit wine or spirits.

Merton Park Golf Links. The Club House.

119 The clubhouse at Merton Park golf course. This private golf course was reached from the southern end of Mostyn Road, and opened in 1912. By 1920 the club had 300 members, paying eight guineas a year, and the course was enlarged to 18 holes in the following year. The attractive clubhouse, built to plans by J.S. Brocklesby, survives as a conversion to several dwellings, in Maycross Avenue, Morden. The club itself was overtaken by the spread of housing, and moved to Morden Park *c*.1933. It seems to have been wound up in 1945.

120 The clubhouse at Raynes Park golf course, *c.*1910. The original clubhouse was in Blenheim Road, but this one, built in 1900, was situated to the west of Grand Drive, in the path of the future Bushey Road. The club, which had opened in 1893, remained here, despite repeated flooding in the early days, until 1925, when it moved to the other side of the Beverley Brook, where it still exists as the Malden Golf Club.

121 Morden Park House, 1950. The fine house of 1770 built by John Ewart, who took a long lease on this piece of the Garths' land, became the club house for a popular public golf course after the last war. It then became parks department headquarters until all council departments moved to Crown House in 1985. At the time of writing it stands empty.

122 Wimbledon Palais, 1979. This building in the High Street, on the site of the Priory gatehouse, opened in 1909 as a roller-skating rink, at the height of what proved to be a short-lived craze. By July 1913 it had become an airship and balloon factory, the rink doing duty as a hangar. In 1922 it reopened as Wimbledon Palais de Danse, and flourished for many years, in wartime there being a special demand. Later it became a venue for all kinds of events, including wrestling and an early Beatles performance, and in its last phase as a place of entertainment it served as a bingo hall. On 1 September 1979 the old rink was reborn as Furnitureland—but what was once claimed to be the largest sprung floor in Europe is still in place!

123 Morden Cinema, 1933. The film titles provide the date of this view of Morden Cinema, which opened in December 1932. Initially independent, it was part of the Odeon group by 1937 and survived until 1973. Three years later it reopened as a DIY store, but it has now been demolished and the site developed as shops and flats. On the extreme right is a corner of the Morden Station garage, now gone.

124 Accordion Club outing, 3 July 1938. There was a craze for the accordion in the 1930s and this club was two years old when 62 members and friends posed for the camera before setting off to Hastings for the day in two motor coaches—with some of their instruments! Behind them is Gosmore, the house built by Bertie White, younger brother of Oscar J. White of Morden Hall Farm, and a popular local figure. This is a late view of the house, which soon afterwards was pulled down to make way for the new Co-op. Mac Fisheries is on the right.

125 Ravensbury Park. The park was acquired jointly by the Merton and Morden and Mitcham Councils when the last part of the Ravensbury estate came on the market, and was formally opened by the Rt. Hon. George Lansbury on 10 May 1930. Boats were available for hire on the mill-pond and were a popular holiday and week-end attraction for many years. This bridge has since been replaced by a less attractive level one.

126 Merton Park Theatre Club, October 1953. A dramatic moment in 'The Thirteenth Chair', performed at the Public Hall, Merton. Many amateur dramatic clubs still flourished at this date, not yet being seriously threatened by television, let alone the video recorder.

127 Tennis at Merton Park, *c.*1950. Tremendously popular, particularly between the wars, tennis was played on public and private clubs much more widely than today. These private courts, on the north side of Erridge Road, closed more than twenty years ago, and were replaced in 1989 by a cul-de-sac of houses.

Shopping

To serve the small and scattered population of the old villages there was a sprinkling of tradesmen, and sometimes tradeswomen. In Merton they were found at the Rush and to the east of the *White Hart*, along Kingston Road and the High Street. By the 1830s there was a choice of grocers, butchers, bakers, drapers and ironmongers; fruit and vegetables, if not otherwise available, would have been bought at the door or grown in the garden. In Morden there may have been one or two shops near the *Plough* and the *Crown*; there was a baker and a grocer near the church, as well as a blacksmith and a wheelwright.

By mid-century Merton had a greengrocer who also sold fish, a market-gardener, shoemakers, a plumber, and a cabinet-maker. And by the 1880s you could bespeak a suit, have your hair cut, buy a watch, a bag of sweets or a bunch of flowers, hire a servant and pick up some medicine.

In Morden Thomas Wilkie Adam established his bakery in Central Road in 1880, on the other side of the road from the *Plough*. By the 1890s there were two other bakers, in London Road, and two general shops had opened.

In the early years of the 20th century shops opened in Nepean Terrace, Kingston Road, to serve the new Bushey Mead estate, and in Seaforth Avenue, as West Barnes began to be built up. A small cluster developed near the *Crown* in Morden, and Mr. Adam's sister, Fanny, opened a stationery shop next to the *Plough* in Central Road.

Many items of food and household goods were brought to the door by cart or van. But, apart from a few specialist businesses, for anything more than fairly basic requirements residents of the area had to go to busier Wimbledon, Kingston or Croydon. This continued to be true until Morden shopping centre developed near the Underground station. By the outbreak of the last war this was large and thriving, with a choice of outlets for furniture, fashions, shoes and carpets, and four retailers with game licences.

Today the pattern of shopping has changed again. Increased use of the car, and the development of superstores on what were once industrial sites in Burlington and Morden Roads have brought hard times to the old shopping areas of Merton and Morden.

128 No.142 Kingston Road, 1913. This 'tuck shop' was run by Mrs. Wheeler and then by Mr. Poore in the old weatherboard cottage from *c*.1905, and the business survived until at least 1940. It was certainly popular with the boys of Rutlish School, which stood on the other corner of Station (now Rutlish) Road. The site of the shop is now the *White Hart* car park.

129 No.49 Kingston Road, *c*.1920. On the Wimbledon side of the road Mr. Baker and his daughter, Marie, stand outside the family sweet shop, which became a general shop in the 1920s. The Bakers were here from *c*.1913 until the 1940s, and the premises survive, little changed, as a lighting business.

130 Kingston Road, *c*.1930. With the development of Bushey Road in the mid-1920s and the prospect of a new railway station nearby in Kingston Road, this parade of shops at the point where the road swings round towards Raynes Park filled up rapidly. From left to right are Edgeller the greengrocer; Dewhurst's butcher's shop; Eyles & Son, grocers, which later became a sub-post office as well; Stowell's off-licence; Eagles' tobacconist, which briefly, as seen here, occupied two premises; Firth's pharmacy; Johnson's ham and beef shop; Thick's dairy (later United Dairies); and Walkley's bakery. Note the early telephone box.

131 No.10 Merton Rush, 1913. In these old cottages at Merton Rush there was once a bakery, and it is thought that Merton's first Congregational chapel was housed in a room here *c*.1818-39. George Nash ran his grocery and off-licence shop from *c*.1890, and with his sons started a building and decorating business *c*.1904. The site was cleared for the Nelson Hospital extension in 1930, when a new off-licence was built, which has now become 'Gardeners' World'.

132 Seaforth Avenue, *c.*1921. This row of shops at the junction with West Barnes Lane began to fill up *c.*1902. From left to right there is J.W. Eve, greengrocer; A.J. Riggs, builder and estate agent; Chamberlain & Hayden, drapers; C.W. Tidman, 'domestic stores'; W.F. Blunden, confectioner and post office; C. Davey, grocer. It was in a room over this post office that the congregation of what was to be Holy Cross church met until the church was built in 1908. At the date of this view Westway would not be built for another nine or ten years, on the open land in the background, across which flowed the Pyl Brook.

133 London Road, *c.*1920. Ernest Chennell, who was enterprising enough to market his own postcard, ran his grocery and post office business in this row of shops in London Road where there was a baker and a confectioner too. Beyond is the old *Crown*, on the site of the present Civic Centre forecourt.

134 London Road shops. Morden's large Co-op was completed in 1940 at a cost of £155,000, taking in the site of Gosmore, Albert Kidman White's house, as well as the original Co-op of 1932. There were 15 departments on three floors, including furniture, millinery, mantles and menswear, as well as provisions of all kinds and a pharmacy, and there was a lift. The Co-op closed in September 1981.

135 Lampert's in 1953. William Waller Lampert began business at 113 Merton High Street as a blacksmith in the 1850s, later being listed as a whitesmith and bellhanger, and gas, electrical and hot water fitter. He served on the local vestry and was treasurer to the lighting inspector. At one time there was a Chelsea branch, but Lampert's remained here in the High Street until the redevelopment of the 1970s. It then moved round the corner into Pincott Road, where it still flourishes after more than 130 years.

136 St Helier Estate shops, St Helier Avenue, 1930. Shops for the new St. Helier estate were an essential part of its layout, and most of the premises in this row were taken early. A cycle dealer, a laundry and a draper opened below the South Suburban Co-op, and between the empty shop and the dairy was a hairdresser, Shears' boot repairs and a sweet shop.

137 Green Lane, 1931. Almost opposite St. Helier station these shops with flats above should have been well placed to serve the south-west area of the estate. United Dairies established themselves early, but some of the premises remained empty for a long time.

138 Central Road, *c*.1935. No longer the village road of even 10 years earlier, Central Road still presented a tranquil scene, and the small child in the road looks safe. These shops below Buckfast Road were at first called Hazelwood Parade, after the house of Hugh Campbell Rutter J.P. which they replaced *c*.1930. When Central Road's numbering system was reorganised they became Nos.44-60. By 1940 there was a grocer, greengrocer, fishmonger, off-licence, chemist, barber and hairdresser here. Note the sign pointing the way to Morden station.

139 Grand Drive Co-op, 1939. With the rapid development in the 1930s of the land on both sides of the Morden end of Grand Drive, a shopping centre was developed just south of Cannon Hill Lane. By 1938 a range of small businesses had opened, even a private library, and in August of the following year a new Royal Arsenal Co-operative Society store was opened. It offered groceries, provisions, meat, poultry, fruit and vegetables, confectionery and tobacco. On the first day Jim Alexander was photographed serving Mrs. Staseby. The potted palms on the counter are probably a special touch for the occasion.

140 Nos.121 and 123, Merton High Street, 1954. These shops, typical of early 19th-century development in Merton, were built as dwellings originally, but around 1900 shopfronts were built over the front gardens. Under various names these two were then occupied by a cobbler's and a sweetshop until they were demolished in the 1970s as part of the redevelopment of the area.

Inns and Alehouses

When we remember that at one time everyone drank ale, as being cheap, nourishing and dependably wholesome compared with either well-water or milk, it is not surprising that every community, however small, had its alehouse or beer-seller.

From Tudor times alehouses had to be licensed by the justices, but the men or women who simply sold beer from their cottages were more difficult to control, and their customers' behaviour to regulate. In a murder trial in 1836 the jury heard witnesses speak of drinking until past midnight at Saunders' beershop, also known as the *Plough*, at Merton Rush, after an earlier long session at the *White Hart*; in his summing-up the judge criticised the practice of paying workmen on Saturday evening in beershops and public houses.

By contrast the business of inns was mainly to provide for the road user—indeed they were obliged to accommodate any traveller. At the *Crown* of the 1830s the public rooms, which included dining-room and bar-parlour, were lit by gas; wine, sherry and spirits were available; and there were beds upstairs.

Situated on an ancient and important highway, the *Crown* did not have to depend for its trade on the villagers of Morden. But there was a small cluster of cottages close by, as also at the *George* and the *Plough*, and at one time there was a drinking-shop at Morden Green to serve the small community there. Similarly 'Lower Merton' had the *White Hart*; the High Street had the *Nelson's Arms*, and at the Rush was the *Leather Bottle*. Between Morden Road and the Wandle there was a wide choice of drinking places. At Raynes Park there was enough demand for the *Junction Tavern* to be built in the 1860s even before the station brought extra trade.

With changes in the law beershops were forced to close or became transformed into off-licences. And with time most of the inns became ordinary public houses. The *Duke of Cambridge* opened on the new Kingston Bypass in 1925; in Central Road the *Plough* was replaced by the *Morden Tavern* on a large site opposite; the *Earl Beatty* and the *Beverley* came in the late 1930s and the *Emma Hamilton* in 1961. Even so, there are today far fewer drinking-places, in relation to the population, than there were 100 years ago.

141 The *White Hart*, 1825. This water-colour drawing by Gideon Yates shows the newly rebuilt inn fronting a narrow rutted Kingston Road. According to the sign the publican was L. Heath, though in the following year Thomas Sutton was here. By the time of the Ordnance Survey map of 1865 the cottages behind had gone and the inn had been extended at the back. The building seems to have survived though altered, and with a bottle department added in 1894, until badly damaged in the Second World War. It was rebuilt early in the 1950s. The *White Hart* formed part of the property left by William Rutlish in 1687 to fund the charity he founded to benefit the poor children of Merton parish. It often served as a public building, accommodating sales, inquests and vestry meetings.

142 The *Dog & Partridge*, 1953. An old ale house which stood back from Merton High Street was established here *c*.1835, the proprietor for many years being James Evance. By 1871 it had become a public house, occupied by James Hudson, and it was rebuilt in 1900.

143 The *Old Leather Bottle*, 1897. There had been a beerhouse here in Kingston Road since at least 1700, and the field that was once behind it was known as Leather Bottle field. In 1898 a new public house was built a few yards to the west, at the Merton Hall Road corner. The old premises became Copus's greengrocery *c*.1900 and survived until *c*.1936. The present carpark occupies the site. On the left of the picture is the Morden Hall Farm dairy shop, which had opened at this corner of the Merton Rush 'island' by 1888.

144 The *Grove* hotel, *c*.1900. Well-placed for passing trade on the Epsom road, the *Grove*, which opened *c*.1862-5, offered accommodation, food, drink and fresh horses. At the date of this view the landlord was Henry George Cockle. The premises were rebuilt in 1912 and refurbished in 1974. A house known as Merton Grove, built by Sir Richard Hotham, once stood nearby, just over the Wimbledon border, approximately on the site of Balfour and Cecil Roads.

145 The *Plough, c.*1920, *left.* In Central Road, once the southern extension of Morden Lane (now Road), stood the modest little *Plough,* which dated from early in the 19th century. At the period of this view it offered teas and accommodation for cyclists. Next door was the stationery shop and post office run by Miss Fanny Adam, whose parrot used to shout 'shop!'. By 1934 the pub had been replaced by the *Morden Tavern,* on a site almost opposite.

146 The *Crown, below left.* There is known to have been a *Crown* in Morden since at least 1801, when a 'new-built' inn of that name was noted. The one in this view, which stood near the junction of Crown Lane and London Road, dated from a rebuilding of *c.*1845 after a fire in 1839 in which an ostler and a 13-year-old postboy died. Although there was talk of an insurance fraud—the sum was £1,000—nothing was proved. The fire may have started in the cupboard where smokers' pipes were stored after a convivial evening, well placed to ignite the tubs of spirits and the stocks of candles which were stored close by.

147 The *Crown, c.*1960, *below.* In 1932 the old *Crown* and the adjacent buildings were replaced by this Tudor-style pub, which offered not only a choice of bars, but a function hall, an off-licence, and an octagonal pavilion for children. Note too the early Mini in this view and that vanished item of street furniture, the police call-box. In 1961 the present *Crown* was built beside Crown House (now the Civic Centre), on the site of the old Village Club, and a Cater's supermarket replaced the buildings in this picture. The site is now represented by the Civic Centre forecourt and the library extension of 1990.

The "George" Inn
EPSOM ROAD
MORDEN, SURREY
Proprietor
Fred Langley
Phones: Mitcham 4216
3513

LOUNGE

SALOON

CAR PARK
FOR 100 CARS

SPECIAL
SUPPER
LICENCE
UNTIL-11. P.M.

LOGGIA & LUNCHEON ROOM

LAWN & GARDENS

148 The *George*, 1930s. The *George*'s appearance has changed many times in its history. Behind the 'classical' façade of this view is a much older structure. A map of 1550 shows a building on the Epsom Road which may very well be a predecessor of this one, and in 1752 the *George* alehouse was described as a timber building with stable and shed, worth £175. Probably originally the *George and Dragon*, it now has a royal George on its sign. Like the *Grove* and the *Crown*, it would at one time have depended largely on travellers on the Epsom Road, and no doubt many horses were rested here after pulling up the George Hill. Fred Langley, who was licensee from 1929 until his death ten years later, enlarged and refurbished the *George* as a typical roadhouse in 1930. In the 1990s, as a restaurant pub with an adjacent motel, the *George* could be said to be a modern coaching inn.

149 No.47, High Path, 1953. There had been an off-licence or ale-shop here for at least 60 years when this photograph was taken. In the background are the brand-new flats of Priory Close, part of the High Path estate.

Wartime

The buoyant mood of the early days of the First World War soon changed, with the shocking reality of the local casualty lists which were published week after week in the *Wimbledon Boro' News*. Merton gloried in the award of the V.C. to Old Rutlishian Lieutenant J.H.S. Dimmer, the first officer of his regiment to rise from the ranks, and in his subsequent rise to lieutenant-colonel. But he was killed in 1918, as was Rev. Richard Colborne, curate at St John the Divine, who had volunteered as army chaplain, and died while ministering to the wounded.

Life was hard at home, too. For families whose wage-earner was at the front or had lost his job in the economic upheaval of wartime the Wimbledon Women's Social and Political Union ('Suffragettes') opened a distress kitchen at 119 Merton High Street, organised by their secretary, Rose Lamartine Yates, of Dorset Hall, Kingston Road, who also set up a clothing distribution scheme. And a Ladies' Committee under Mr. H.H. Holland, council chairman, raised and distributed funds to relieve local distress. Many people began to grow vegetables, and there was a thriving Pig and Livestock Society.

Schoolchildren sometimes brought shrapnel into the classroom. But the Great War left few physical traces in the area—although a defence structure in London Road survived for many years as Searchlight Cottages. Morden commemorated her fallen with the lychgate of 1920, and Merton's war memorial was installed in 1921 at the corner of the churchyard.

Preparations for the next war began early. With the alarms of 1938 came gas masks, first-aid classes, trenches in every park, and searchlights at the new Civil Defence centre in Dorset Road. By mid-1939 there were 38 Air Raid Precaution wardens' posts being built.

With the outbreak of war in September 1939 the schools closed. Two evacuation zones, both in Merton, had been agreed: the Bushey Mead and Polytechnic estates, and the industrial area near the Wandle. The children who stayed did lessons at home, until school air-raid shelters had been built and the schools could re-open. Local Defence Volunteers (who became the Home Guard) installed concrete barriers in main roads. A gun site and command post was built in Bushey Road; a food control office was installed in St Mary's church hall and a mortuary in Joseph Hood Recreation Ground.

The Blitz began locally on 16 August 1940, when a number of bombs fell near Merton High Street and the Wandle, killing 19 people and damaging many buildings. Between then and May 1941, most parts of the district suffered. There were then few incidents until June 1944 and the first V-1, or flying bomb. Thirty-five of these fell on Merton and Morden between June and August, killing 60 and injuring about four hundred. Boys at Rutlish School, which lost its science block and junior department, had some of their lessons at the Old Rutlishians' pavilion in Poplar Road. About

16,000 houses were damaged and 275 families made homeless. Empty houses were requisitioned for them as well as for refugees.

From the outset morale was recognised as important. Municipal concerts and 'Holidays at Home' were put on at Mostyn Gardens, on a stage constructed over the air-raid shelter. In the warm weather there was dancing at Moreton Green and the recreation grounds.

Four British Restaurants were opened, to supply low-priced basic meals, off the ration, mainly for workers, and in some cases for schoolchildren. Four nurseries were opened to enable mothers to carry out factory and other essential work.

'Dig for Victory' allotments were laid out on many of the district's open spaces, and pigs were reared in Garth Road. 'Warship Week' in 1942 raised £230,000 from the people of Merton and Morden for HMS *Acute*. A 'book drive' for the forces brought in 70,000 volumes. And everything that could be saved for salvage was saved.

150   In July 1918, when King George V and Queen Mary made a visit to the area especially to see wartime gardens and allotments, the Merton Church of England Boys' School gardens were chosen for royal inspection. Outside the school a guard of honour stood to attention in front of the King, in a top hat, and the Queen, who holds a bouquet of carnations presented by the Girls' School. In the school log book, in red ink, Mr. Johnson the headmaster wrote:

Their Majesties the King & Queen, amid the loyal manifestations of the children, and other inhabitants of Merton, visited our School Gardens... The Chairman of the Urban Council, the Chairman of the Agricultural Committee and I were then honoured by being presented to Their Majesties the King and Queen, Whom I escorted through the School Gardens. On leaving The Royal Visitors expressed to me the interest They had experienced.

151 Merton Park allotments. The site was owned by the Merton Park Estate Company and lay just to the west of Poplar Road. The allotments opened on 1 January 1912 and were visited by the King and Queen on the same occasion in 1918 as the royal visit to the school gardens. Wartime brought greater demand for allotments and increased powers for local councils to negotiate with owners of suitable land. During the hard times that followed the end of the First World War the allotments became even more necessary, and these plots survived until the end of 1925 and the development of Poplar and Erridge Roads. In the distance are the chestnut trees of Kenley Road.

152 Morden Hall military hospital. In the First World War Gilliat Edward Hatfeild's Morden Hall became at his wish a military hospital. There were 68 beds, and, as the men regained strength, they had the freedom of Hatfeild's park. After the war Morden Hall became an annexe to the London Hospital, receiving women and children as patients. The hospital closed in 1941, with the death of Mr. Hatfeild.

Mrs. Gladstone's Convalescent Home Mitcham.

153 In 1915 Steel Hawes, in Central Road—also owned by G.E. Hatfeild—was opened as The Grange by its founder and matron, Mrs. Lewin, as a military hospital with 34 beds. Here, *above left*, some of the patients are taking the air. After the war The Grange became a nursing home, and continued as such until 1964. Ten years later it nearly became a pub but, having been rebuilt and extended, it is now company offices.

154 Ravensbury Park House which lay close to where Seddon Road meets Bishopsford Road, was built in 1864 for George Parker Bidder, the railway engineer. In 1900 it was taken over by the Catherine Gladstone Convalescent Home (founded in 1866 by the wife of the statesman, William Ewart Gladstone), and for the duration of the First World War it operated as a military hospital. In 1923 it became an annexe of the London Hospital, administered by the 'Marie Celeste' Samaritan Society, receiving women and children as patients. After bomb damage in the 1940s the house was demolished. This view, *left*, dates from before the First World War and, despite the caption, the house was in Morden.

155 The signing of the Treaty of Versailles on 28 June 1919 was the signal for spontaneous celebrations all over the district, with street parties, fireworks, singing and flag-waving. The people of Gore Road held this children's party, *above*, during a sunny evening of a much longed-for day. At this date the west side of Gore Road near Approach Road was not built up, and there was plenty of space for a street party.

156 Air-raid precautions at the John Innes Horticultural Institution, 1938. The staff can be seen installing one of four air-raid shelters in the Institution's trial grounds, close to the main buildings. The site today is occupied by some of Rutlish School's buildings; the distinctive wall runs beside the path between John Innes Park and the recreation ground. The war closed the Institution's chemistry laboratory, but despite the bombs (including eight V-1 rockets in 1944) work of practical importance as well as some theoretical research was achieved. By October 1944, 40,000 copies of six information leaflets had been distributed to nurserymen, market gardeners and fruit growers.

157 An Easter wartime wedding held in the garden of Newlands, 2 Dorset Road in 1940, and despite the anxious times everyone has a smile for the camera. The bride's brother and two of his friends were on leave from flying Hurricanes with 238 Squadron, Manston. Over the fence can be seen The Oriels, 146 Kingston Road, which stood between Newlands and the level crossing. It was damaged in an air-raid in August of that year and was subsequently pulled down. Dating from the mid-1880s it had once been the home and office of John Innes' architect, H.G. Quartermain, who had designed it and Newlands. Its last occupants were Finch & Co., estate agents, who then moved to premises on the Wimbledon side of Kingston Road.

158 'A Corner of Merton, 16 August 1940'. Artist Harry Bush lived at 19 Queensland Avenue, one of Brocklesby's houses, with a large studio on the top floor. This was his view on a day when a group of Junkers planes dropped bombs on and near the oldest industrial area of Merton. His detailed painting shows the neat crater in the centre of chaos. On the left behind the houses in Bathurst Avenue is domestic debris of all kinds, including a mangle; Brisbane Avenue beyond is virtually unaffected. In the bottom right-hand corner can be seen an Anderson shelter, with thriving vegetable marrow plants on top.

159 'Evening Incident', 16 August 1940. In Bathurst Avenue a *Times* photographer caught the blown-out windows, the wrecked Ford 8 and the shrapnel littering the ground. Have all those onlookers just emerged after the 'All Clear'?

160 A narrow escape, 1940. The *News Chronicle* commented that no-one in a shelter was injured when this bomb fell just behind these maisonettes in Runnymede, making a crater that can be seen behind the two women and the small boy. The date was 16 August 1940.

161 The scene here is of Liberty's print works at Merton Abbey, on 16 August 1940. The large building is the 1929 Shop and in front is the works office, with the screen store on the extreme right. Despite the damage work returned to normal almost immediately. All the buildings were repaired, and the 1929 Shop survives as part of the Merton Abbey Mills Market complex, though the small buildings were demolished in the 1980s.

162 The end of a Junkers 88 on 20 September 1940. The plane was hit by anti-aircraft fire over south London, lost height rapidly, dived over Wimbledon and crashed into Nos. 2 and 4 Richmond Avenue, Merton. One crew member, who had baled out over Clapham, landed on a roof and gave himself up; the others died in the crash. ARP rescue workers are on the scene.

163 The Home Guard on parade at Dorset Hall in Kingston Road. The hall had been owned by the Council since 1935 and at the outbreak of the Second World War it housed the Clerk's Department and the Air Raid Precautions Officers. The premises and grounds were regularly used for ARP and Civil Defence training but the once fine lawn was obviously not a wartime priority!

164 Bomb damage in Dupont Road, 1940. The Bushey Mead estate, close to the main railway line and densely built-up, was one of Merton's evacuation zones and received several hits, during the Battle of Britain in 1940 and again in 1943. These houses were early casualties, when a stick of bombs fell on the estate. They were not rebuilt until after the war.

Local Government

The origins of local government can be seen in the rôle of the churchwardens as it developed from the Middle Ages onwards. It was they who raised the church rate for repair and upkeep of the fabric and fittings of the church, and often distributed alms to the poor, even before they assumed official responsibility for poor relief in the 16th century.

With time the vestry system developed. All male ratepayers could attend meetings (held by tradition in the church vestry, though in Merton they often adjourned to the *White Hart!*), and began to take on more and more duties. The members appointed from among themselves Overseers of the Poor and Surveyors of the Highways, unpaid but quite onerous posts, and out of the rates they paid small stipends for the services of a constable, a sexton and a parish clerk. The manor was responsible for the pound and the cage, and appointed its own constable and common-keeper. A manorial ale-conner regulated the quality of ale brewed in the manor.

During the 19th century new bodies were set up to administer local affairs. The parishes of Merton and Morden were placed under Croydon Poor Law Union and Croydon Rural Sanitary Authority, while the local Highway Board was at Kingston. With the creation in 1889 of the County Councils, it was recognised that some powers should be delegated locally, and in 1894 the secular rôle of the vestries was transferred to new elected parish councils. At the same time rural and urban district councils were created. John Innes, who had been defeated in the first county council election, failed also to have Merton, where he was lord of the manor, made an urban district. The parishes of Merton, Morden, Mitcham, Beddington, Woodmansterne, Coulsdon, Sanderstead and Addington, and the hamlet of Wallington were placed under the administration of Croydon Rural District Council.

In 1907 Merton finally achieved urban district status, and in 1913 Merton and Morden came together when they were granted permission to amalgamate as Merton and Morden Urban District.

The Council ran its own fire brigade and its own ambulance service, and opened maternity and child welfare clinics—the first two at High Path and Raynes Park. Having inherited an unregulated mixture of dwellings, shops and businesses, particularly in the High Street area, it had to deal with nuisances caused by smoke, effluent, smells and noise. In Morden such operations as pig-rearing, tallow-manufacture and bone-steaming were confined to the area of the old common, which developed into the Garth Road industrial estate.

The Croydon Rural Sanitary Authority works, built in 1877 at Byegrove Road, drained the district. They were enlarged and improved many times and became the Wandle Valley Sewage Works. In 1907 a pumping station had been built beside West Barnes Lane to provide drainage for development in western Merton.

The first recreation ground to be opened in the district was Nelson Garden in 1908, on land once owned by Admiral Isaac Smith of Merton Abbey. On the other side of

Morden Road the Abbey Recreation Ground, bought before the First World War, had to remain as allotments until 1924. Over the years several other open spaces were acquired, the largest being 48 hectares (120 acres) of the Morden Park estate, bought with help from the Surrey County Council soon after the Second World War.

Between the wars the population of Merton and Morden grew faster than in almost any other part of Greater London, and the Urban District became one of the largest in the country. By 1939 the council was pressing for incorporation as a borough, but with the outbreak of the Second World War the matter had to rest.

In the end it was with the boroughs of Mitcham and Wimbledon that Merton and Morden were united as the London Borough of Merton in 1965. Merton gave its name to the new borough; Morden has since 1985 housed the council offices, and since 1990 the council chamber.

165 Hoardings in Coombe Lane, 1911. The proliferation of advertising hoardings along the tram route, where it ran past the open fields of West Barnes Lane into Coombe Lane, was a frequent cause of complaint. The council tried to control the spread, while local landowners awaiting the right time and price to dispose of old farmland saw it as a useful temporary source of income, and the Water Board permitted hoardings along its strip of land in Coombe Lane.

166 New housing, 1923. J.W. Ellingham of Dartford produced this advertising postcard when he worked as principal contractor for the first phase of Merton and Morden's Whatley estate, in which local architect Sydney Brocklesby was concerned. In the central foreground is the John Innes Recreation Ground and its pavilion and just to the left Whatley Avenue strikes out towards Martin Way and open country beyond. The Raynes Park Schools, Haynt Walk (named after an old wood), Botsford Road and Mawson Close (named after Isaac Mawson Brash, chairman of the housing committee) occupy the middle ground, and Bakers End is in the bottom right-hand corner. In 1929 the Wimbledon-Sutton railway line was constructed to cut through between Mawson Close and Bakers End. In the top right-hand corner is Bushey Mead, which gave its name to Bushey Road and to the development now more often called the 'Apostles'.

167 Culverting, 1925. The western part of Merton was notoriously badly drained. In 1925, in an effort to solve the problem for good, new pipes and culverting were put in from near Botsford Road, through Bushey Mead, across Carters Tested Seeds trial grounds, beneath the railway lines and onward to the Beverley Brook at Coombe Bridge. The work, subsidised in part by the Unemployment Relief Scheme, was completed in February 1926 at a cost of £63,557. Power Petroleum had premises facing Carters across the northern end of West Barnes Lane c.1925-31, but the large shed shown here seems to have stood on the piece of land enclosed by the two railway lines serving Epsom.

168 Flooding in Lower Morden Lane, *left*. The flat and low-lying ground of Lower Morden, which has clay soil, drains only gently towards the Pyl Brook and always used to flood after rainstorms. The Raynes Park golf club regularly complained to the council about sewage on the fairways; and here a sheet of water in Lower Morden Lane extends into the Battersea cemetery. The cemetery, which opened *c*.1890, lay on land purchased from Hobald's Farm.

169 The cemetery, July 1938, *below left*. In 1938 it was agreed with Battersea Borough Council that Merton and Morden and Carshalton Councils should take over for their own use some surplus land at Battersea's cemetery in Lower Morden Lane. Landscaping and road construction began at once and the architect's plans were drawn up to include a chapel and other buildings. The cemetery opened for burials in 1940, but the outbreak of war brought all sorts of building work to a halt, and it was not until 1955 that the chapel was finally built. In the background is the chimney of the Garth Road refuse destructor.

170 Merryweather Fire Engines, 1926, *below*. In the yard at the Kingston Road council offices stand both old and new machines belonging to Merton and Morden Fire Brigade. On the right is the Merryweather vehicle bought in 1910 by the then Merton Urban District Council for £784, after a demonstration of its pump and hoses at Liberty's premises on the Wandle. On the left is the newly purchased machine of 1926, also from Merryweather & Sons. It had a Hatfield reciprocating pump and cost £1,400. Note the one-time Morden Hall Farm Dairy shop, which had only recently been taken over by United Dairies.

171 The opening of Morden Recreation Ground, April 1926, *above*. This was Morden's second recreation ground, purchased with the proceeds from the sale of the original one, which had been given to the people of Morden by G.E. Hatfeild in 1913. This one had been part of the Lodge Farm estate, and lies south of Central Road. Hugh Campbell Rutter J.P., a member of an old Morden family and a councillor, performed the ceremony at the main entrance.

172 Morden Recreation Ground, 1935, *right* Gardeners are at work and a cyclist keeps to the path as the notice instructs, in this view looking towards Central Road.

173 Joseph Hood Recreation Ground, 1926. Joseph Hood, Member of Parliament for the Wimbledon Parliamentary Division, gave £11,000 to buy and prepare for use a site in Cannon Hill Lane as a recreation ground, which was opened by him in 1921. Here Sir Joseph Hood, Bart., as he had become, delivers the first bowl on the new bowling green on 1 May 1926.

174 A view of Cannon Hill Lane, beyond Martin Way, in August 1927. This second phase of housing for Merton and Morden went up in 1927, on part of the residue of the Whatley estate. It was completed in time to claim the full government subsidy, and the houses were occupied as soon as they were ready.

175 Garth Road Depot, *c.*1938. Refuse dumping for the district was first carried out at an old gravel pit in Morden Road and then at the old brickfield site off Green Lane (later Martin Way). After a short period of tipping at Baron Grove, Mitcham, a new site was opened in the early 1930s in Garth Road. The original horse and cart service had been superseded in 1919 by two electric vans, which proved less reliable and economic than hoped, and in 1926 the council bought its first tractor and tipping trailer. Four Morris refuse vans were bought in 1939.

176 A council meeting in session on 28 March 1949. Between 27 May 1942 and the formation of the London Borough of Merton in 1965 Merton and Morden District Council meetings were held at Morden Hall, in more spacious surroundings than the old chamber in the Kingston Road building.

177 The Hatfeild Mead housing development of 1953, built between London Road and Central Road, was named to commemorate the last lords of the manor of Morden, the Hatfeild family. The architect was A.J. Thomas. Before the Second World war the area of land, known as Site 'H', had been envisaged as a site for a large new civic centre.

178 Pincott Road, 1961. Rebuilding of the High Path neighbourhood was begun in 1953 with large 'closes' of flats near Morden Road. This is one of a series of photographs taken by the council's health department in 1961 to illustrate the old, decayed and insanitary housing which was being replaced.

179 Nelson Grove Road, 1961. These early 19th-century cottages, among the more substantial housing in this part of Merton, are towered over by the new flats of Priory Close. The notice on the wall with directions for G.W. Shotter & Son is a reminder of a notable episode in local history. In 1894, in the first election for Merton Parish Council, George William Shotter, black-smith, was top of the poll, beating the 'gentleman' candidates and trouncing the vicar into eighth place. So remarkable was this considered that the national press featured the story and *Punch* honoured Mr. Shotter with verses beginning, 'Over the vicar, top o' the tree, The Village Blacksmith stands ...'.

180 The old library at Raynes Park. In Aston Road in 1931 Surrey County Council opened a library and a dental clinic in this building, originally a temporary school of 1906. Only 3,000 books were provided for a readership that reached 4,500 in six months, and the book stock had to be doubled. Furnishing was done on the cheap and included a green enamel counter. For a time during the last war the library was housed in shop premises at 570 Kingston Road while the ARP used this building. It was not until 1967 that Raynes Park had a new purpose-built library.

181 West Barnes Branch Library, 1956. This corner shop at 359 West Barnes Lane was converted in 1947 to a library, which in 1976 was replaced by a purpose-built library off the main road.

182 Merton and Morden Central Library, 1950. The old council offices in Kingston Road, built by Merton Parish Council in 1903 and enlarged in 1911 and again in 1930, were left nearly empty by the Council's move to Morden Hall in 1942. The central library, which had been housed in the old Masonic Hall since 1933, was moved here, releasing the hall for use as an all-purpose public hall. The move was achieved in 1942, and the library remained here until new premises opened in Morden Road in 1960. As Morden Library it moved again in August 1990 to the new extension at the London Borough of Merton Civic Centre in London Road.

183 Ever since the formation of Merton and Morden Urban District in 1913 there had been pressure to provide a swimming pool. Plans were interrupted by the First World War, by the hard times that followed, and again in 1939 by the outbreak of the Second World War. It was the London Borough of Merton which built these baths as one of its earliest projects. They were opened in 1967 by Lord Hunt, who had led the successful Everest expedition of 1953.

Bibliography

Chamberlain, W.H., *Reminiscences of Old Merton* (1925)

Denbigh, Kathleen, *History and Heroes of Old Merton* (1975)

Jowett, E.M., *A History of Merton and Morden* (1951). This remains the standard account

Jowett, E.M., *Raynes Park* (1987)

Livermore, T.L., *The Story of Morden and its Churches*, 2nd edn. revised W.J. Rudd (1983)

Prentis, W.H., *Snuff-Mill Story* (1970)

Spencer, C. and Wilson, G., *Elbow Room* (1984)

Wallace, John, *Dorset Hall in Merton* (1991)

Wallace, John, *Long Lodge at Merton Rush* (1993)

Wallace, John, *A Walk Around West Barnes*, 2nd edn. (1987)

Wallace, John, *Spring House* (in preparation)

Collections at Morden Reference Library, Wimbledon Reference Library, Surrey Record Office, the John Innes Society and the Wimbledon Society

Publications by the John Innes Society and Merton Historical Society

A series of articles in *Merton and Morden News*, 1973-4, entitled 'The Merton Story'

Note: Morden Library has large collections relating to the two most celebrated figures associated with the district, Horatio Nelson and William Morris.